*Al & Sally
Thank you sooo much
for all you are and do for
our local community & church overall*

GOD Has GREAT Plans for You!

A Guide to Help Clarify Your Calling and Increase Your Happiness

God bless you

by Joseph Michael Tabers

D1281856

Discover
Learning

Ann Arbor, Michigan

Discover Learning Registered Number –

ISBN # 978-0-9702220-4-6

P.O. Box 130857
Ann Arbor, Michigan 48113

Phone: 734-332-8770
Email Address: greatplans@discover-learning.com

Book Cover, Illustrations and Text Design by Ewa Krepsztul
Earth Photo courtesy of NASA

Editing and Creative Input by Karen Walker
Walker & Associates Strategic Communications

Category: 1 Self-Help, 2 Vocation, 3 Vocational Guidance, 4 Job Satisfaction,
         5 Work-Religious Aspects-Purpose, Christianity

Dedication

To my two wonderful sons...Michael and Gregory.
May you both discover and act on God's great plans for you!

And in memory of Sr. Mary St. Catherine,
of the Monastery of the Blessed Sacrament,
Farmington Hills, Michigan,
our Aunt, encourager and prayer warrior,
with love.

To you, the reader...

All of us have moments of clarity
where God's plans for us, seem very clear.
We also have times when fog sets in,
where we can't see what's ahead.
Our job is to take the first step or two
when clarity is present,
trusting in good faith that
He will lead us through the fog.

Joe Tabers, author

No matter who you are or where you may be, you can do something to change the world for the better!

Father James Keller, founder of The Christophers

WHY THIS BOOK?
A word from the author

My name is Joe Tabers. As of this writing, I am 50 years old. Since my 17th birthday a quick 33+ years have gone by! (I'll share more about myself later). Looking back, I wish I'd had a book like this when I was in my teens or early 20s. I'm sure this book would have helped me get a jump-start on discovering my mission in life and ways to make more of a positive difference in the world.

That's why I wrote this book, first to help you get a jump-start in discovering the type of vocation and work God may be drawing you toward. Second, to assist you, a friend or family member, in learning more about your unique strengths, dreams and capabilities so that you may grow into the best person God wants you to be!

In these pages, you will find:

- Encouragement and answers leading you to greater happiness, peace of mind, and the discernment of God's will for you.

- Inspiration that will keep you inspired about the value of choosing a life of service that benefits other people.

- Thought-provoking questions and worksheets to give you clarity as you think about, plan and discern your life's calling.

When I was 17 years old, I was a pretty observant kid. Just by reflecting on how many times I had been protected from the stupid mistakes and close calls that most kids make and we somehow survive, I knew, trusted and believed that God had plans for me – even at age 17! Of course, what exactly those plans were, I wasn't so sure. But one thing was for sure…my calling started to become clearer when I began to do my part to pay attention to and take inventory of the gifts and the signs that God had been sending me along the way. Since I am a bit of a slow learner, it took me a while but…I finally learned that the more I worked, talked with and co-operated with God, the clearer His plans became!

This book can help you do the same thing, to gain a greater understanding into what type of work, vocation, or calling God may be drawing you – a calling you can remain passionate about the rest of your life!

Of this you can be certain…no matter who you are, where you are, or what mistakes are in your past…GOD LOVES YOU! AND GOD HAS GREAT PLANS FOR YOU!

If you have any doubts about this, ask God right now to reveal those plans to you. Do this and you will benefit, even if this is the only fact you remember from this entire book!

Table of Contents

"*The world offers you comfort, but you were not made for comfort, you were made for greatness.*"

Benedict XVI,
during his first week as Pope

INTRODUCTION

A s a young adult, chances are pretty good that you've probably been asked these kinds of questions before:

> So, what do you want to be when you're out of school?
>
> Have you decided what you want to do with your life yet?
>
> In what kind of work/career do you see yourself?

...And your response, like mine, probably has changed a bit over the years.

Let's face it: The answers aren't always clear to us...Sometimes these questions are just annoying. Sometimes you may feel like you have an answer. Other times, deep inside, you honestly wonder what the answer is for you!

As a young man growing up in a small town just outside of Detroit, I was asked these same questions from relatives, neighbors and friends of my parents.

Like most kids, I wondered and imagined what it would be like to do different things for a living – to be a firefighter, a police officer, a doctor, a teacher, or maybe a soldier or a jet pilot! After all, one of the purposes of our imagination is just this, to try different things on "for size" and imagine how that role or type of work might (or might not) suit us as something we could see ourselves doing later in life.

When I was in my teens, some of my young friends would say... "Wouldn't it be cool to be a rock star or a professional athlete for a living?" Other kids would mention a particular career and say, " That job pays the big bucks, now that's what I want to do!" But me, I admired those people who seemed to know that for which they were best suited...you know, those individuals who seem to be perfectly cut out for what they do. I didn't know why at the time, but I was drawn to those types of people. They seemed to be sincerely happy, and they exuded a real joy for life and for other people. *That's* what I wanted!

But how did these people get there? How did they know what career or vocation was right for them? And how could I find out what career or calling was right for *me*? That is the aim of this little book – to share with you things I have both researched and discovered along the way that have helped me clarify my purpose, my life's work, and my vocation/calling. The tools and insights in this books have helped many others I've met over the years to discover their calling too. Now, more than ever, I am confident that these pages can help you, a friend, or a family member to do the same!

Yes, GOD does have great plans for YOU!

Following the examples and written exercises in this book can help you to discover what HIS great plans are for you.

WHAT MOVED ME TO WRITE ABOUT THIS TOPIC?

For the past more than 20 years I have worked as a professional speaker and corporate trainer. This work has allowed me to travel to nearly all 50 states and four countries. This work has also given me an unusual opportunity to work with literally thousands of people from an amazingly wide variety of careers and vocations. My role was, and often still is, to conduct a series of interactive workshops that help improve business communication, leadership and teamwork skills.

At the organizations and companies where I led workshops, the hard-working people who attended came from hundreds of different types of roles, careers and occupations, many of which I never even knew existed! I have had the privilege of meeting, working with and learning from many of these terrific individuals. I learned about what they do, how they do it and even how they got started or interested in their field or calling.

As I've grown to better appreciate God's plan in my own life and as I've seen His plan lived out in the lives of hundreds of others, I've come to appreciate how great a role faith and spirituality plays in the daily workplace.

All too often a certain type of work or vocation is perceived in a negative light, usually by others who either don't understand it or know much about it. In reality, work is a gift from God and a great benefit for us all. John Paul II said it well when he wrote in 1981, *"Life without work is deformative and through work man becomes a more human being, more dignified and more noble, if he carries it out as God intends he should."* (*Laborem Exercens (On Human Work)* is an encyclical written by Pope John Paul II in 1981)

By investing just a few minutes in each of the following chapters, you will gain insights to see and understand more clearly what God has uniquely created <u>you</u> to do in life. You will learn ways to make a positive difference serving others right where you are or wherever He may be leading you.

In order to help you discover God's great plans for you, be sure to do the exercises marked **YOUR TURN** ╱ . Also answer the questions in this book candidly, from your heart. Those answers are there, right now inside you, waiting to be discovered more fully! So grab a pen or pencil and...

LET'S GET STARTED!!

OBSERVE, ADMIRE, LEARN
From the Best Around You!

When people tell me that they've learned from experience, I like to say that the trick is to learn from other people's experience.

Warren Buffet,
U.S. investor, businessman and philanthropist

Exercise care in what you watch. It is estimated that up to 73% of what we learn, comes to us visually. Choose to see the good, the wonder and the awe in all of God's creation...including His people.

Joe Tabers

He glanced up and saw the rich putting their offerings into the temple treasury, and also a poor widow putting in two copper coins. At that He said: I assure you, this poor widow has put in more than all the rest.

Luke 21:1

Do you understand what I just did for you? You address me as teacher and Lord and fittingly enough, for that is what I am. But if I washed your feet – I who am teacher and Lord – then you must wash each other's feet. What I just did was to give you an example: as I have done, so you must do. I solemnly assure you no slave is greater than his master; no messenger outranks the one who sent him. Once you know all these things, blest will you be if you put them into practice.

John 13:13-17

It was in about eleventh grade when I had a spirit-led observation and discovery. I began to look around more closely at the people in my life - parents, teachers, relatives, neighbors, friends and even acquaintances. I observed and was fascinated by the profound differences in how people lived, worked and interacted with others.

Some might say this is just part of growing up, but for me it was a memorable observation. This simple observation changed me. It changed how I looked at people. It made me think about what was possible for my future. That's why I share it with you.

You see, for the first time in my life,

I asked myself, of the people I know...

- Who seemed the happiest?

- Why were they happy?

- Who didn't seem happy or fulfilled?

- Why not?

- Why did they like (or not like) their work or their state in life?

YOUR TURN /

If you haven't asked yourself these questions, try it!

To begin, see if you can come up with a list of, say, five to 10 people you know. Write these names (or initials) in the left-hand column below:

5 to 10 People I know:	Observations:
1.	
2.	
3.	
4.	
5.	
6.	
7.	
8.	
9.	
10.	

Now, if you're like me, you'll notice whether there's a trend, a pattern among the 10 people whose names you wrote down. Look at this list and ask yourself: Who seems the happiest/most fulfilled? Why? Or Why not? Do each of these people seem to love what they are doing? Why or why not? Who seems most at peace? Jot your observations to the right of the list above.

DISCOVERING CORE QUALITIES I ADMIRE IN OTHERS

When I began reflecting on the lives of my aunts and uncles, neighbors, fellow students, and so on, it inspired me to take a closer look at myself.

It's surprising but true – a few minutes of serious reflection like this can change your life. I know it can, because it changed mine! One Saturday afternoon when I was 17 years old, I sat at the picnic table in my parents' backyard. I had a blank notepad and an issue of *Success* magazine. The magazine had a section about creating a blueprint for your life. A blueprint for my life? That sounded great to me!

Three and a-half hours later I was on fire with written pages of things I wanted to do, have, be, and become. The bottom line is that you wouldn't be reading this book now if I hadn't dreamed, planned and written things down that day, over 30 years ago!

YOUR TURN ✒

So, let's continue. Go ahead! Don't worry about getting this book marked up, that's what it's for. Some of my favorite books are highlighted and filled with many hand-written notes, key points and underlines. This book is for you to do the same!

List the names of three people you most admire and respect.

1.
2.
3.

My first list of three people I admired and respected included 1) My Dad, Hank, 2) A wonderful, encouraging Dominican nun named Sister Mary Louis, and 3) A gifted local radio talk show host personality named JP McCarthy.

Next, I asked myself (and I recommend you do as well): **What are two or three common denominators that I admire about these three people?**

List the COMMON DENOMINATORS that you admire about these three people:

I still remember that on my list years ago, quickly I wrote:

> 1. Sincerity.
> 2. They care about and respect other people.
> 3. They each work to make a difference in the world by "who" they are, and "wherever" they are.

"That's it!" I thought after completing the list.
I can choose to duplicate the qualities and virtues that I admire most in others.

This realization motivated me to dig even deeper.

My research continued. I hope yours will too, using the next several pages...

CREATE YOUR SUCCESSFUL TRAITS LIST

Review the short lists you have just made. Look at the shared common denominators you observed in the three or more people you most admire. Now think more deeply about these observations and write a more expanded list of shared traits that you've observed in the happiest people you have met or know. Compare this list with another list that you will create, namely, a list of the most restless people you know. Write down the common traits of the most restless people you know. Compare the two lists. These lists can be extremely helpful, as you will see later on.

One important word of caution: While it is OK to mentally reflect on some of the qualities of your least favorite people, people whom you may choose to avoid, it is never a good idea to make a written list of names of people that you do not admire or respect. Why not? It's because we each have imperfections too. And we're each called by God to show dignity to one another. We don't have to necessarily love all that someone does, but we can still respect the person and leave the final judgments to God. As it is said: *Love the sinner. Hate the sin.*

Besides, we usually have enough work to do on improving ourselves, let alone worry about trying to change or improve others (which rarely works anyway!). Also, it doesn't accomplish much for us to focus on others' imperfections and weaknesses. At best, all this does is remind us of behaviors we don't appreciate. At worst, it causes us to rush to judgment or cynicism. A waste of energy indeed! Our goal here is to observe common positive traits or virtues we CHOOSE to duplicate.

On the next page is my original "successful traits" list.

When I finished reflecting on the lives of other aunts, uncles, neighbors, fellow students, and friends, here's what else I discovered:

JOE'S RESEARCH LIST
What I Observed and Learned about People

THE HAPPIEST AND MOST FULFILLED SEEM TO:	THE LESS HAPPY, RESTLESS, AND LEAST FULFILLED SEEM TO:
– Be sincere	– Be insincere, disinterested
– Give you their full attention	– Be critical/cynical of others
– Care about others, help, share	– Be selfish/don't offer a hand
– Forgive others' mistakes/ shortcomings	– Be quick to judge, condemn
– Enjoy and show interest in people	– Blame situations and people for problems
– Treat you as if you're important	– Come across as self-promoting
– Respect and trust others	– Display apathy, indifference or low-energy
– Take personal responsibility	– Listen poorly or sporadically
– Be upbeat, easygoing	– Show little or no effort to practice faith/belief
– Be able to laugh or make light of themselves	– Pray only when desperate, or not at all
– Be confident, yet humble	– Be boastful, proud
– Compliment and encourage others	– Rarely keep promises/commitments
– Believe in and talk with God	– Appear interested in self and getting vs. giving
– Trust in God and most people	– See self-sacrifice as troubling (to be avoided)
– Practice/exercise faith & prayer	
– Express gratitude, gratefulness	
– See self-sacrifice as greater good (embrace it)	

YOUR TURN /

Now it's **your turn** to create your own Successful Traits list.

Reflect on the lives of your aunts, uncles, neighbors, fellow students, and friends and start writing behaviors/actions you observe:

YOUR RESEARCH LIST
What You Observed and Learned about People

THE HAPPIEST AND MOST FULFILLED SEEM TO:	THE LESS HAPPY, RESTLESS, AND LEAST FULFILLED SEEM TO:
-	-
-	-
-	-
-	-
-	-
-	-
-	-

This list was the beginning of an exciting journey to improve areas in my own life. Did you see some of the shared qualities I saw when I did this comparison? What qualities can you observe within your own list that you would like to duplicate?

I am convinced that anyone can benefit by taking a few minutes to observe, admire and learn from others. Learning from the beauty of other people's experiences and wisdom can help us to grow and improve.

If you haven't already written a list like this or if it's been awhile, take the time right now to do it. I am confident that **if you are willing to make a list of your own right now, it will be a valuable experience for you as well. Model yourself after the best!**

MAKING IT YOUR OWN

O nce you've completed your list, begin with the happiest side and ask yourself...

>   1. How many of these behaviors do I already practice in my day-to-day approach with others?

>   2. Which one or two behaviors do I want to cultivate within myself?

For example, on my list, two behaviors that I already practiced were: "Interest in other people" and "being upbeat". Those traits come easily for me because I like people and I am optimistic.

On the other hand, some of the qualities I needed to work on included, "being more sincere with others" and "trusting more in God's will for me". Since I like being in control, the behaviors I needed to work on also included "the ability to laugh at myself more"–"to have greater humility"– and "not to take myself so seriously."

TURNING YOUR OBSERVATIONS INTO ACTIONS

Y ou know how it is. Observation is one thing, even the very profound observations and discoveries made in the last few pages. But if these observations aren't put into practice in your daily life, then discovering God's great plans for you will be much more difficult. In other words, virtuous behaviors lead to virtuous results.

As long as I can remember, I have liked the saying "actions speak louder than words". In fact, during my first supervisory job I placed a 3 x 5 card on a wall board that read:

DEEDS
AND NOT WORDS...
ARE WHAT COUNT MOST.

No matter how we describe it, the critical point is to put these observations into do-able actions. Let's do that now.

YOUR TURN /

Take out a 3 x 5 card and write down (from your last list) two or three good traits that you have right now. Also write down two or three traits that you will commit to work on... Do It Now!

This little 3 x 5 card, that easily slips into your purse, wallet or on your bedroom mirror, is a powerful tool. Each day, and even several times a day, take out your 3 x 5 card and review it. How are you doing today?

Most of us don't change overnight. We change incrementally. But you will see, over time, that little by little, the traits that you admire – the few that you wrote down on your 3 x 5 card – will become easier to practice and more of a part of your own natural style. After awhile, other people will observe and find those noble and good traits in *you*; the same traits that you only saw in others whom you admired before!

THE VALUE OF ASKING AND THE LAW OF "INVITATIONS"

What do your actions invite into your life? If you don't pay attention to the little things, you might be surprised one day to find yourself where you don't want to be!

Little things add up over time to become good (or bad) habits. What do you invite into your life by your actions *right now*?

While working as a teenager and taking some early college courses, I earned money by doing janitorial and building maintenance work at a nearby monastery. When I was 18, I saw an ad for a one-day "Custodial Training Course" offered by a local supply company.

I asked my employer if I could attend. To my surprise they not only agreed to let me go on paid work time, but also paid for the course fee as well. During that workshop, I learned some valuable lessons that still are with me today, many years later!

This was one of the first adult training workshops I'd ever taken and I was so impressed by how much someone can learn in a one-day workshop! I learned smart, time-saving and labor-saving methods. I learned the power of "visual invitations" as applied to keeping things neat and orderly. For example, if you leave paper on the ground, next to a trash can, it "invites" more misplaced trash. And if a sign is worded "Thank you for not smoking", it will generate more cooperation than a NO SMOKING sign ever will.

Not only did I gain new insights on how to be better at my building maintenance job, I also learned how to be a better thinker and leader. I still remember and use one of the handouts we received that day. It was a poem entitled *Sermons We See* and it is still one of my favorites. As you will see when you read it, this simple poem lays out the characteristics and habits of a true leader.

After you read the poem, ask yourself, whose actions do I follow? What actions does my life model for others? What actions or reactions – good or bad – do I "invite" into my life by my current choices or actions toward others?

Sermons We See

I'd rather see a sermon
    than hear one any day.

I'd rather one should walk with me
    than merely point the way.

For the eye's a better pupil
    and more willing than the ear.

Fine council is confusing,
    but example is always clear.

And the best of all the preachers
    are those who live their creed.

For to see the good in action
    is what everybody needs.

I can soon learn how to do it
    if you let me see it done.

I can watch your hands in action,
    but your tongue may too fast run.

And the lectures you deliver
    may be wise and true,

But I'd rather get my learning
    by observing what you do.

For I may misunderstand you
    and the high advice you give.

But there's no misunderstanding
    how you act and how you live.

Edgar Guest

LEARNING FROM INSPIRING WORDS

In addition to learning from the habits and actions of people around us, we will explore how words - both written and spoken - can inspire us to see God's plan for us as well!

Around the age of 17, I began to read and learn more about the amazing powers of our mind, and about how our thinking and our words impact our actions and results.

The human mind is incredibly powerful. It turns words into images. Our job is to take good care of what images we allow to enter and occupy our minds.

For example, in my bedroom when I was a teen and young adult, I would put up selected words and posters to inspire me. One of the posters I still remember vividly had a beautiful mountain scene and the words: *All that I have seen teaches me to trust the Creator for all that I have not seen.* I still get inspired just recalling that poster.

Yes, research has proven, and I firmly believe, that we need to choose wisely what we repeatedly reflect upon or what we allow our minds to dwell upon.

The late Dr. Maxwell Maltz, in his book *Psycho Cybernetics*, states that "the mind cannot tell the difference between a real and a vividly imagined experience".

In another example below, taken from the writings of the St. Paul the Apostle, we see just one of the many wise Scripture passages upon which we can meditate with impressive results that will impact both our heart and our spirit. St Paul writes:

Whatever is true,
whatever is honorable,
whatever is just,
whatever is pure,
whatever is lovely,
whatever is gracious,
if there is any excellence and
if there is anything worthy of praise,
think about these things.

Philippians 4:8

Christ is called "the living Word come down from heaven". All we have to do is study, savor and meditate on the words that Christ spoke, recorded in Holy Scripture, and strive to live them in our lives - to "rest" in His words. The Holy Spirit will then inspire us and help us to take Christ's words and put them into action. In other words, we do our part...and God does His part.

INSPIRING WORDS CAN INFLUENCE PRIORITIES, BELIEFS AND ACTIONS

In addition to reading the Bible for God's great words to live by, we can also get and stay inspired by surrounding ourselves with beautiful art, quotations, and posters with soul-stretching words by other great men and women - especially the saints - throughout history!

I believe that everyone should surround himself with a personal collection of inspirational quotes, poems and verses. Below, and throughout this book, are a few of the many inspirational verses I continue to collect even to this day. Consider using some or all of these quotations as a start (or an addition) to your own collection of inspiring quotes and verses.

The only things that endure beyond time and into eternity... are those things done with selfless love.

Fr. Robert Werenski

One the most beautiful compensations of this life is that man cannot sincerely help another without helping himself.

Ralph Waldo Emerson

I have made my chief study in the book of Charity; it teaches everything.

St. Dominic

A hundred times every day I remind myself that my inner and outer life depend on the labors of other men, living and dead, and that I must exert myself in order to give in the same measure as I have received and am still receiving.

Albert Einstein

Man's actions are the picture book of his creeds.

Ralph Waldo Emerson

Faithfulness, not success is all that God asks of us.

Mother Teresa of Calcutta

The habit of insisting upon the best of which you are capable, and of always demanding of yourself the highest, never accepting the lowest, will make the difference between mediocrity or failure, and a successful career.

Orison Swett Marden

I long to accomplish a great and noble task, but it is my chief duty to accomplish humble tasks as though they were great and noble. The world is moved along, not only by the mighty shoves of its heroes, but also by the aggregate of the tiny pushes of each honest worker.

Helen Keller

Happiness does not come from having, but from appreciating what you have. Joy is the fruit of appreciation.

Matthew Kelly

Do not fear; only believe and [all] shall be well.

Luke 8:50

Do not be anxious about anything, but in everything, by prayer and petition with thanksgiving, present your requests to God. And the peace of God which transcends all understanding, will guard your hearts and your minds in Christ Jesus.

Epistle of St. Paul to the Philippians 4: 6, 7

SUMMARIZING THE TAKEAWAYS

So, in a nutshell: How do I observe, admire and learn from the best?

Remember:

✓ **Be Clear.** We become more like the people we respect and admire...so be clear on the qualities you respect and admire in others.

✓ **Choose to be Self-less.** Notice that the most inspiring people of the past have consistently been those who are more self-less versus selfish.

✓ **Pick good friends.** "Show me your friends...and I'll tell you what you're like," says Sister Mary Louis DeMonfort, O.P.

✓ **Read the best.** Learning from the best requires reading the words written by or about the best.

Chapter 1 Action Tips:

○ **Read your 3x5 "traits" card daily.**

○ **Collect inspiring words and quotes,** and surround yourself with them.

○ **Read a page a day.** Begin today to read at least one page a day of inspiring words. A great place to start is with the Gospel of John.

Now that you have reflected upon the strengths of the people you admire, it's time to reflect upon your own strengths!

Chapter Two

REFLECT ON YOUR PRICELESS GIFTS: Stay Grateful!

Gratitude is the sign of noble souls.

Aesop (620-560 BC)
Greek author, Aesop's Fables

We can either be our best cheerleader or our own worst critic.

Joseph M. Tabers

Consider the lilies of the field, how they grow; they toil not, neither do they spin: And yet I say unto you, That even Solomon in all his glory was not arrayed like one of these.

Matthew 8:28-29

Our gifts spell out our responsibilities.

Monsignor Clark

J ust as other people who do good works can inspire us, so also, we too can inspire others by our good works.

But no one can give inspiration to others unless he first has inner inspiration himself. That means that before you or I can inspire others, we must first be inspired ourselves.

And one of the most fundamental ways to fill our souls with genuine inspiration is by first recognizing and expressing gratitude for God's incredible goodness to us and for us. Taking stock of what you and I have going for us - thanks to God's goodness - builds powerful momentum and excitement. And it is grounded in reality, humility and truth, not on false thinking or pretension.

I remember that at my high school graduation party, which was held at my parent's home, mom and dad's best friends, Bea and Lenny, gave me a graduation card with a poem by Amanda Bradley.

I still remember how interested Bea and Lenny were in me, how happy they were for me, and how much they believed in all the possibilities that my future held. Their words of encouragement, coupled with that graduation card and the poem it contained, would become inspirations that remained with me for years. Following are the words of that special graduation card:

FOREVER AND ALWAYS, BELIEVE...

Believe in yourself,
what you think, what you feel,
Believe in the truth,
in the good, the ideal,
Believe that your dreams
can someday become real...
Forever and always, Believe.

Believe in yourself
and in what you can do.
Believe in the goals
that you strive to pursue.
Believe in the friends
who believe in you, too...
Forever and always, believe.

If you use each today
as a chance to reach out,
To learn something more
of what life's all about...
If you follow your dreams,
strive to make them come true –
then life's sure to bring
all the best things to you.

Amanda Bradley

Yes, this gift, and Bea and Lenny, were great encouragements to me. What a difference sincere encouragement of others can make in our lives...I know it did in my life!

And today, some 30 years later, having met thousands of people in business and in life, I'm still convinced that we all need to express gratitude and share encouragement - for our own strengths and talents, as well as for those of others with whom we live and work.

Regarding our own strengths, the good news is that we don't have to wait around for others to provide recognition or encouragement. I believe that we all benefit by sitting down and reflecting on what we have, instead of on what we don't have. Whenever we take the time to sincerely appreciate the strengths we have been blessed with , we grow in confidence and generosity with others.

DON'T SELL YOURSELF SHORT!

That little inner voice of self-criticism and self-doubt can be louder than the truth! Too often we knock ourselves down or sell ourselves short, especially as teenagers. But it even happens as we get older, especially as we reach higher, stretch beyond our "comfort zones" and try new things, new directions.

We sometimes worry about being accepted, fitting in, or what others may think of us. Even as adults, we can be too negative with ourselves and our "self-inventory". If you ever catch yourself doing this...Stop! Refocus on what you have and not on what you don't have...Yes, you really do have a lot going for you! Thank God today and often...You'll be glad you did.

THE SURPRISING REALITY

I was made aware of how we tend to sell ourselves short while speaking to a group of teens at a high school one day. I was talking about the power of clarifying your purpose in life.

Everything seemed to be going great – everyone was interested and engaged. But then, in the course of my talk, I asked the students to do something very simple. The results surprised me.

I asked the students to take out a piece of paper and number the left side from one to 10, and then, quickly, to write down three to 10 of their strengths, skills or positive qualities that came to mind. I walked around the room, glancing at the students' writings. After a few minutes, I noticed that most students still

had a blank page! Only a handful of students had written one or two attributes. No one had written even three of their strengths!

After further encouragement and prompting, with suggestions such as "How about your smile?" "Are you a hard worker?" "A good friend?" "Good at math?" Eventually, a few students wrote one or two more things.

But I knew that each teen in the room had so many more gifts and talents than he or she recognized! What could I do to help the students see this?

I decided to try a spontaneous experiment. I asked the students to turn their papers over and on the back side list a few of their weaknesses (talents they lacked). To my amazement all of them quickly started writing! Quickly, each of these students wrote down three to 10, even more than 10 qualities that they lacked!

When I later asked these students why they found the second task of writing weaknesses easier than writing their strengths, they responded in unison: "It's easy to write down what you're not good at!"

That's when it dawned on me that not recognizing our good traits and talents is both a blessing and a problem. It can paralyze us and prevent us from moving forward.

How is it a blessing to know our weaknesses? When we know that we're not cut out for something or not best suited for it, this can keep us humble. It prevents us from saying "yes" to things too quickly. In such cases, God may want us to seek the help of others or to sign-up for additional education or training. Or, He may want us to stretch out of our comfort zones for the greater good of others and work on developing a new skill or ability.

How is it an immobilizer to know our weaknesses? When we dwell on our weaknesses too long or too often, we begin to falsely believe that we are not good at anything. But in reality, nothing could be farther from the truth! You are unique in all of the universe.

The simple truth is this: *There is not another YOU! There never will be another you either! There is not another individual in the whole world, in the whole of history, exactly like you!*

Yes, you are absolutely unique and yes, *you* **were born to do great things!**

Consider this...

You-YES, YOU! - are Fearfully and Wonderfully Made!

Yes, you truly are "fearfully and wonderfully made", as the Psalmist wrote. Scripture also records that "every hair on your head is counted". Somebody carefully made you and He loves you *more than you can possibly imagine!*
Think about what that means...

You, a mere human being, are a son or daughter of God. As a child of God, you obviously have self-worth, as well as the capability and even the responsibility to do great things now and in the future.

The great things you are called to do might turn out to be, as Mother Teresa said, "little things done with great love".

But if you don't recognize what you are called to do, using all of your unique combination of gifts and talents, there will be an emptiness in the world somewhere...And the places and people you alone could touch and reach, will not receive what only you could bring them, through God's grace.

It's pretty amazing, isn't it?!
So, let's discover *your* unique combination of priceless gifts...

TAKING INVENTORY OF YOUR STRENGTHS

YOUR TURN /

To begin your "priceless gifts" self-inventory, ask yourself some basic questions and write out your answers as they come to you *without over-analyzing* – Just Write!! Here are some great questions to begin:

– What am I good at, or best at, right now?

– What type of work do I most enjoy doing?

– What comes easy for me?

– At what have other people told me I am really good at or a "natural?"

– What do I get most excited about doing or working on? What brings me interior satisfaction?

– What keeps coming back to me as something I "must" do, or something I feel compelled to finish?

– How might this work or calling benefit other people?

In case you want to see the results of my list, from more than 30 years ago, here's what it looked like:

MY SAMPLE LIST OF STRENGTHS AT AGE 17:

What am I good at, or best at, right now
Helping people   Learning
Fixing things   Encouraging others
Exercise

What comes easy for me?
Trouble-shooting (finding and fixing problems)
Seeing the good/potential in others

What do I get most excited about doing or working on; what brings me joy or inner satisfaction?
A job well done
Improving/repairing things
Helping others
Making the world better

The answers to each of these questions can lead us to try a certain type of work or job for awhile to see how we like it or how it "fits" us. Our first job(s) can also be a great way to try different things, to discover what we do well, and brings us greater joy?

For example, I knew I was good working with my hands, fixing things. I had earned a state mechanical certification in high school, fixing cars, so upon high school graduation, I went to work at a major car dealership for six months. I was 18 years old. On that job I learned a lot of great things and was inspired by some really good, highly skilled people. I also witnessed some examples of poor attitude and poor work ethic and things I did not want to emulate. It was on that first job where I learned that even though one can make a good living as a mechanic, it was not what I felt called to do.

YOUR TURN /

FINDING WHAT "FITS" FOR YOU...

B elow you'll see some reflections designed to be thought-provokers, just to get you thinking about some possibilities and opportunities that perhaps you might not have considered before. It's a quick overview, not too detailed, but I hope it be helpful in your discernment process.

YOUR VOCATION

K eep in mind that your "Vocation" is not necessarily the same as your "Calling", even though the word "vocation" comes from the Latin word for "to call".

That might sound confusing.

Here is the bottom line: There are two main levels to God's call for each of us – The level of "Vocation", or "state of life", and the level of specific skill set, aptitude and interest.

At the level of "Vocation", God calls some of us to become priests, religious sisters or brothers. He calls others to be mothers, fathers, or single men or women. These different states in life – married, single, priest, or religious (which means belonging to an order of priests, brothers or nuns) – are designated by the Church as different "Vocations".

YOUR CALLING

Within each Vocation, there are what I refer to as different "callings". So, for example, a young woman may be called by God to be a nun, but not any kind of nun, a missionary nun, or a cloistered nun, or a teaching nun. The vocation in this example is to be a woman religious, but the specific way an individual is called to live out her vocation is different for each person.

The same is true for a priest or brother. A young man may be called to serve God in the vocation of priesthood, or as a religious brother, but he may feel called to become a medical priest, or a parish priest, or teacher brother.

And, for those whom God calls to live married or single lives, clearly there are specific choices and callings that include spouse, career, family goals and so much more.

Of course, God draws us toward his plan for our lives in his own way and timing, and in the way that is best suited to us. Many times we discover our Vocation and calling at the same time, in the same discernment process. Other times, it takes longer to discover, or we discover it in stages, over a period of time.

THE STORY OF ONE CISTERCIAN MONK

To give you a fun example of one young man whom God called to serve in a monastery, consider Fr. Bernard McCoy, O. Cist. As of this writing, Fr. Bernard is the prior of Our Lady of Spring Bank Monastery in Sparta, Wisconsin. He is also a pilot, and the founder and president of an online e-business, called www.LaserMonks.com, that supports his monastery. But if you went back to see what Fr. Bernard was like as a teenager, he had no idea he was going to become a monk. In fact, he wasn't even Catholic!

As the youngest of two boys, the future Fr. Bernard was very interested in business and astrophysics. In his teens, he earned a financial planning certificate, ran a business fixing computers for several schools, and was also an outstanding French Horn musician in an orchestra. He entered college early, at only age 16, to pursue a degree in astrophysics.

But before the end of his first semester, the future Fr. Bernard felt very unsatisfied. He sought something more, something deeper than what his college experience promised. Through a remarkable set of "coincidences", he ended up transferring to a small Catholic college that was a four-year Great Books college, on the other side of the country.

Prior to this, Fr. Bernard had never even met a Catholic before, and he'd never been further west than Georgia! Can you imagine?! But, as some people observe, there are no coincidences in life.

LaserMonks.com

God had a plan for Fr. Bernard, just like He has a plan right now for YOU! In Fr. Bernard's case, he ended up converting to the Catholic faith his first year of college. He also ran an import/export business out of his dorm room the first two years of that same college. Keep in mind, there were no cell phones then, and no computers, only faxes, snail mail and one central dorm phone! He quit the business cold in his second year and began focusing more on his studies. By the end of his senior year, he knew God was calling him to "be on the other side of that altar," as he puts it.

After much searching, after college graduation, he felt strongly that God wanted him to be at the Cistercian monastery in Sparta, Wisconsin. It's not the choice he would have made initially, but he strongly felt like it was what God invited him to embrace. He went through an extensive formation period at the monastery, studied in Switzerland at the monastery's Mother House, got a Ph.D., and then returned to the Wisconsin monastery to live his life as a monk. Soon after returning, he was asked to develop a business for the monastery so that it could sustain itself. While exploring different business enterprises, including some with less than desirable results, Fr. Bernard launched LaserMonks and, with the help of some friends, it took off!

In the example of Fr. Bernard, you can see how God gave him, at a young age, an interest and talent in business ventures and music. Then God called him first to one college, then another. He called him to become a Catholic, to drop his extra business activities, and ultimately to the vocation of priesthood. And then God wonderfully used this young man's particular talents and skills within his priestly vocation!

As you can see, the discovery of God's plan for YOU can take place a little at a time. So you may as well enjoy the journey!

SOME CONSIDERATIONS...

To help jog your thought process about what naturally attracts you, here are some questions to think about:

- Do you like working with your hands? Your head? Your heart?

- Do you enjoy working with (or without) people?

- What kind of challenges do you enjoy?

- What problems do you like to help solve?

We've discussed the three primary states of life, or Vocations. Here is a partial list of some of the many, many possible callings within those vocations. Circle which callings initially interest you, and cross off which ones seem definitely not for you:

Dentist	Lawyer	Electrician
Doctor	Auto Mechanic	Accountant
Nurse	Sales Professional	Musician
Engineer	Teacher	Banker
Scientist	Artist	Coach
Lay Minister	Counselor	Architect
Builder	Entrepreneur	Business Owner
Writer	Editor	Professional Speaker
Researcher	Skilled Tradesmen	Financial Planner
Painter	Beautician	Dietitian
Fitness Expert	Technology Expert	Veterinarian

For additional areas of vocational interest and helpful resources be sure to visit our website at **www.GodHasGreatPlans.com**

A FEW MORE GOOD REFLECTION QUESTIONS TO CONSIDER:

- Who am I?

- Why was I created?

- What am I supposed to do with my life?

- What could I keep doing for hours and still enjoy it, or the challenge of it?

- Does who I am and what I do right now have significance in the life of at least one other person, and maybe in the lives of more than one person?

- Is what I am doing this very moment helping others?

INSPIRING FACTUAL ANSWERS TO REFLECTION QUESTIONS:

When you ask yourself...

Who am I?

Remember:

- You <u>are</u> a son or daughter of God.

- You are unique in all of creation, "handmade" in every detail for a greater purpose.

- Your life is an unrepeatable miracle!

- THERE WILL NEVER BE ANOTHER YOU.

- You are a son or daughter of your parents.

- You may be a brother or sister to a sibling or several siblings.

- You are also a cousin, friend, neighbour, student, employee, or co-worker.

- And, at some point in your life, you are, or probably one day will become someone's uncle or aunt.

Why was I created?
Remember:

- You were created to do great things, even if those "great things" are simply "little things with great love".

- You were created because of God's great love for you.

- You were created to grow in knowledge, love and grateful service to God in this world, and to prepare for eternity with Him in heaven.

- You were created to live with God forever in the next life — WOW! Just keep this in mind and you'll stay focused on what's truly important in your life!

What must I do?
Remember:

- Become the best you that you can be.

- Seek to do God's will in all ways and in all things.

- Love and serve your neighbor as yourself.

GOING FORWARD

G od indeed does have great plans for you. As you read further in this chapter, keep in mind these helpful facts:

- You are created in the image and likeness of God. (Genesis 1:26)

- You are fearfully and wonderfully made! (Psalm 139:14)

- "God meets our needs in order to free us to meet the needs of others." (Fr. Jim Meyer)

- Gratitude is the fuel that gets our motor running.

- Knowledge and appreciation of self is one of the prerequisites of greater knowledge and appreciation of God.

GRATITUDE PROPELS US FORWARD TO SERVE OTHERS

W hen we recognize how blessed we are, how many gifts we have been given, we cannot sit still. The love of Christ propels us forward in gratitude to serve others.

There is always unseen power in counting your blessings. Remember, "an attitude of gratitude" is welcomed just about everywhere.

KEEPING AN ATTITUDE OF GRATITUDE CAN SEE YOU THROUGH ROUGH TIMES!

T o give you an example that illustrates what a big difference it can make in your life to always keep an attitude of gratitude - even in tough and challenging times - let me tell you about a rough spot in my life...

It was 1984. I got married, moved and started a business all in the same year. That year was a happy, exhilarating blur. But looking back years later, I remember how tough things got for me. By then I was fixing up our house and trying to run my new business out of that same house.

My business was, and still is, providing leadership and team communication training to the employees of companies that hire me. One day I was the person standing in front of people as a leader and trainer, and the next day I was doing grunt work at home, fixing the house and doing the laundry downstairs.

As you can imagine, during the days of slow business and house work, I was overwhelmed and plagued with nagging self-doubt. A myriad of questions danced in my head. I kept wondering to myself – "Why bother? Am I really making that big of a difference anyway?" and "I'm so overwhelmed, why not throw in the towel and just get a regular job?"

This frustration and self-doubt might not seem like a big deal now, as you read it. But at that time for me, let me assure you, it was HUGE.

You see, I was at a place that we all experience at different times in our lives. I could not see the light at the end of the tunnel! Should I continue to pursue this speaking/training business I felt called to, or not? I had to walk in Faith and Hope, but I didn't realize it. I just felt overwhelmed.

I couldn't see the big picture, the full reality of my situation with God's eyes. I would later learn to step back and see the big picture more often, and encourage others to do so as well.

TRUST IN JESUS - NOT IN OUR OWN LIMITED EFFORTS

One day a few years ago, it dawned on me why we struggle with self-doubt when we get overwhelmed and overworked. It was a huge relief to discover this answer, and that's why I share it with you now. Hopefully you'll remember it when you hit these overwhelming times of self-doubt and questioning in your own life!

I suddenly recognized that the devil, the Liar of liars, (and yes the devil is real) can plant those self-doubts in our minds to discourage us. Prayer and the Holy Spirit counters those temptations to despair with drops of hope, according to the ways we best will receive it.

Here's the great part...when you and I catch on to The Liar's methods, we can more easily brush our fears aside and go forward, trusting in Jesus for our success, and not trusting in ourselves alone!!

YOUR TURN /

1. When we focus on the things for which we are most grateful, we always receive newfound encouragement and energy to carry on. Take a moment right now and list on a 3 x 5 card (or wallet-sized piece of paper) at least three things for which you are most grateful. Do not over-analyze, just write three things. Keep this card in your wallet or purse. Whenever you take the time to read or add to this simple gratitude list, you'll smile and be glad you did!

2. Keeping our attitude in good shape is another practical way we can counter self-doubt. The self-assessment that follows will help reinforce 10 ways you can exercise the strength of a good attitude when facing the daily challenges of life.

TAKING INVENTORY OF YOUR OUTLOOK/ATTITUDE

Assessing and Learning from Your Past Behaviors

> *I believe one of the most important qualities for success in life and work is choosing and maintaining a good and grateful attitude.*
>
> Joseph M. Tabers

MEASURE YOUR APPROACH TO LIFE AND TO SITUATIONS

Following is a brief self-assessment that can help highlight your strengths as well as some areas where you need improvement. Circle the number that best represents your current performance.

Rate yourself from   **5** = I am **excellent** at this,
          to   **1** = I am **poor** at this.

		Exc.	Good	Avg.	Fair	Poor
1.	I am an active self-starter/go-getter every day.	5	4	3	2	1
2.	I regularly choose to be grateful and to make the best of each day.	5	4	3	2	1
3.	I verbally express my gratitude to God and other people on a daily basis.	5	4	3	2	1
4.	I am good at teamwork, helping others, pitching in, and supporting others' efforts/work.	5	4	3	2	1
5.	I am good at focusing on other's strengths and good qualities and not dwelling on their weaknesses or shortcomings.	5	4	3	2	1
6.	I usually avoid giving excuses and refrain from blaming others for things that go wrong.	5	4	3	2	1
7.	I regularly operate by the belief that I can choose my attitude and responses to most situations.	5	4	3	2	1
8.	I work at communicating with my fellow students/coworkers both in providing information/ updates and in asking for information as needed.	5	4	3	2	1
9.	I am good at addressing differences of opinion without criticizing others, spreading rumors, or creating unnecessary tension in relationships.	5	4	3	2	1
10.	I accept criticism gracefully, without over reacting or quickly denying it, but instead using the best of it to improve myself.	5	4	3	2	1

TALLYING IT ALL UP

A s with the other self-assessments in this book, consider also asking a friend, co-worker, parent or boss to rate your behaviors as well. Now add together your circled ratings.

The top score is 50. **If you score 42 or more** you have an exceptional attitude. You are likely a blessing to have around. Again, you might consider asking a few peers to score you to see if they agree. Few people are consistently in the top category (42 to 50).

If you are in the 33 to 41 range, you have a pretty good attitude. Even so, ask yourself what it would take to make a current rating of 2 or 3 on one item you circled into a 4 or 5?

If you scored 24-32, it's time to start working at improving your attitude now. Your friends, family members and others will someday thank you!

If your score is 23 or less, no matter how well you are doing in the other areas of your life or job, you'll need to improve your attitude dramatically – and quickly.
Make a decision now to continue to read, learn and keep growing.

But don't worry. You are never alone, some of the greatest saints in history overcame the most miserable attitudes and negative inclinations…keep reading…

IF YOUR ATTITUDE DOES NEED FIXING…

H umble yourself and ask God for His help now. Commit to setting aside a little quiet time every day to read Scripture and reflect on it. Actually, setting aside this quiet time every day is absolutely essential to inner peace and growth, no matter what your score!

Also, reading one of the many great books on the topic of attitude can help us approach things differently. One such book to consider is *Winning Ways, Four Secrets for Getting Great Results*, by Christian business author, Dick Lyles.

The qualities of good attitude and behavior are just as important to you as good food and rest. You already know that if you eat junk, you will feel junky. If you are not at your best, get some rest.

IF YOU SCORED HIGHER...

Now, you might be tempted to think that if you scored 40 or higher, you don't need to do much...But that would be like an Olympic swimmer deciding he did not need a coach because he had already won a few big medals. Or, like a musician who did not think she needed to keep practicing.

Remember, attitude is a choice, a daily choice, a split-second choice. And it takes constant vigilance and humility (through recognizing you can't do it alone), to maintain a healthy, inspiring attitude. Good attitude is a habit that grows stronger over time, with ongoing practice.

IF YOU SCORED 30 OR UNDER,
THERE'S STILL GOOD NEWS...

If you scored 30 or under you might be tempted to think you're a failure and don't have a chance. But this isn't true at all!

Remember when I mentioned that some of the saints overcame the most miserable of attitudes? In a sense, they were lucky because there was no way that they could ignore their own reality. Their faults and bad attitudes became so obvious (and obnoxious) to themselves, that they clearly recognized their need for constant reliance and trust in Divine help to overcome them, one day at a time, one incident at a time, bit by bit. The more these future saints messed up, the more they prayed for help…and you know what, even when they had left their bad attitude in the dust, so to speak, they kept on daily, hourly, constantly praying for help to be better.

If you need some examples on great saints who overcame great obstacles in their attitudes, read as much as you can about the great St. Jerome, who was said to have had a terrible temper; or St. Augustine, who struggled for years with his attitude toward self-gratification and sins of lust and the flesh; or St. Francis de Sales, who was by nature very impatient but who eventually became so tempered this trait that by the end of his life he was known as the most gentle of men; or even St. Teresa of Avila, who had to deal with complacency early in her consecrated life.

Yes indeed, the attitude that you and I practice daily – with God's constant help – is the one that defines how effectively we let God achieve His purposes through us, today and in the future.

HELP COMES WHEN WE HANG IN THERE, TRUST AND LISTEN…

So, back to that frustrating time in our laundry room when I felt like giving up on my dream of speaking and working with audiences. It was in the midst of that uncertainty that I recall whispering a prayer "Lord what do you want me to do?"

Moments later I was given a clear ray of hope, a crystal clear thought that I quickly wrote on a piece of paper nearby. Soon after writing and reading it, I had an immediate sense of its truth and value. I placed a copy of it on my office wall. That little inspiration has served me well over the past 25 years.

I titled that inspiration "Choice Not Chance" and I share a copy of it with you here in the hope that it may inspire you as well!

CHOICE NOT CHANCE

You were created to do great things...
to make a difference in this world.
Only you have your unique combination
of experiences, skills, talents, and gifts.
How you choose to use these...
to best serve God
and to benefit other people
will directly determine your level of
happiness and
your personal success.

Joseph M. Tabers ©1989

SUMMARIZING THE TAKEAWAYS

So, in a nutshell: How do I grow in gratitude that inspires me?

REMEMBER:

✓Work at becoming and remaining your own best cheerleader - after all, you are made in God's image!

✓You are a son or daughter of God!

✓Know that you are created to do great things! (Even if they are little things done in a great way!)

✓God has given you a unique set of experiences, skills, talents and gifts - unlike the combination He has given to anyone else in history and unlike any He will give to someone else in the future. Allow your appreciation for these gifts to impel you forward.

CHAPTER 2 ACTION TIPS:

○ **Carry it with you.** Reflect on and carry with you in your wallet a short list of the things that you are most grateful for in life.

○ **Be grateful every day.** Give thanks every day for the things, situations and people you like, and for the ones you are not as crazy about. Remember, God has a higher plan - a plan to bring you blessings!

○ **Inspire at least one person every day.** Other people can be inspired by your gratitude and thankfulness; simply by observing and benefiting from your attitude of gratitude!

ASK AND LISTEN FOR GOD'S GUIDANCE:
Seek His Will

There are only two important things in this life: sincerely seeking and doing God's will in your life. Pray for both...especially for the strength and focus to do the latter.

> Fr. John Hardon - Born: June 18,1914
> Ordained a Priest: June 18,1947
> Entered into Eternal Life: December 30, 2000

What you wish for and hope for is small compared to what I have planned for you.

> God
> from the book *Our Father*, by Matthew Kelly

Eye has not seen, ear has not heard, nor has it even dawned on man what God has prepared for those who love Him.

> 1 Corinthians 2:9

For I know the plans I have for you declares the LORD, plans to prosper you and not to harm you, plans to give you hope and a future.

> Jeremiah 29:11

I can still remember some of my favorite prayers during my late teens. Many of them I still pray today as an adult. Here is one of them... *The Mother Stuart's prayer:*

PRAYER OF MOTHER STUART

Keep us, O God, from all pettiness.

Let us be large in thought, in word, in deed.

Let us be done with fault-finding
and leave off all self-seeking

May we put away all pretense
and meet each other face-to-face,
without self pity and without prejudice.

May we never be hasty in judgment,
always generous.

Let us take time for all things,
and make us grow calm, serene, and gentle.

Teach us to put into action our better impulses,
to be straight-forward and unafraid!

Grant that we may realize that
it is the little things of life that create differences,
that in the big things of life we are one.

And, Lord God, let us not forget to be kind!

Some say that God's favorite prayers are the prayers we pray for others, not for our own needs. In my life I've noticed this to be true many times. In hindsight, most of the prayers I prayed for others were answered in one way, shape or form.

Of course, our prayers are not always answered the way we want or expect. But they are *always* answered the way **God** knows is best.

Yes, sometimes it's easy to accept God's answer to our prayer, and other times we struggle or get angry at the answer we receive.

But I can say with absolute confidence as I look back over my life, and prayers of the past, that even when I got answers I didn't want to hear or experience, God's way was much better for me than my way would have been!

GOD ANSWERS ALL OF OUR PRAYERS - IN HIS OWN WAY

Here is an example of a difficult time in my life when I did not know what God wanted, but I sure knew what I wanted! When I was a teenager, my mother could have died from heart problems. It was something I often prayed about as a teen. Yet by God's grace, mom is still with us, more than 30 years later!

I can still remember sitting by mom's side at 2:00 AM in the pre-dawn cold and darkness. We were on the living room couch. I was about 12 years old at the time. My mom was crying and holding her chest. She was scared because the pain was so bad. I was scared too at the thought of losing her. Mom refused to let me call an ambulance and didn't want me to wake up dad to take her to the hospital. She didn't want to go to the hospital. I think that's because she thought at the time that if she went to the hospital she may never come back. So we just sat there together and I rubbed her back...feeling helpless and scared. "Pray, Joey, Pray!" mom told me.

So I prayed as a 12-year-old would pray, straight from the heart, simple and direct, silently asking God for His will. My prayer went something like;

> Dear Lord, please help mom.
> If you really need her, go ahead and take her
> but we'll miss her dearly.
>
> Could you please wait till we are grown up
> and don't need Mom as much as we do now?
> Thank you Lord. Amen.

Somehow it all worked out. God answered our prayer as He saw fit, and as I said earlier – more than 30 years since that cold, frightening night on the couch, my mom is still with us.

A very different example of one of my prayers is a time when I prayed for meaningful work that would help a lot of people. I am sure the work that I do today as a professional speaker working with audiences and helping them improve their leadership and relationship skills, is an answer to that prayer from my teens.

I also prayed specifically for my vocation. I think this is one of the most important prayers we can make. God has made each of us for His purposes, and to some of us He gives a very special call to become a priest or religious sister or brother. It's important not to drown out such an invitation with distractions, and to support those who are considering or testing whether indeed such a beautiful vocation is what God has in mind for them.

For me, I prayed that if marriage was to be my vocation, that God would bring me to the right woman, a woman with many of my mother's generous qualities. Within three or four years Betty came into my life, another answer to my simple and intense prayer in my parents' backyard on a beautiful summer night, 26 years ago.

One of my favorite prayers during the Mass is when the priest says 'Father, almighty and ever living God. We do well always and everywhere to give you thanks...' Just think, God is ever present to us – always and forever, no matter what our circumstances or where we are! He is always present to us if we but look for Him in:

- Prayer
- The Mass
- The Sacraments
- Tabernacles worldwide
- Other people
- Our soul
- Scripture, which is His Living Word

We just need to do our part (like a radio receiver) and tune in!

PRAYER REALLY DOES MAKE A DIFFERENCE!

O f this you can be certain, just as temperature and molecules change water from a liquid or gas into a solid, so too does prayer change the course of things in our lives, and in the lives of others.

As the famous poet Lord Alfred Tennyson put it,

> More things are wrought through prayer than this world dreams of.

Father Patrick Peyton, the famous priest who held Rosary Rallies for thousands of people around the world in the 1940s and '50s, often quoted Lord Tennyson's words. And with good reason.

Against all odds, Fr. Peyton gained access to public radio airwaves and even television to broadcast a family and movie stars praying the Rosary. Against even more odds, he enlisted famous Hollywood actors and actress of the time, like Bing Crosby and many many others, to pray the Rosary, sing sacred songs, read scripts for family-friendly radio drama, and film re-enactments of Christ's life and events recorded in Holy Scriptures.

Fr. Peyton also had Rosary Rallies in the United States, the Philippines, South America and in other cities worldwide. Held in giant sports arenas and stadiums, Fr. Peyton's Rosary Rallies drew crowds up to 5 million at a time. In fact, he became a household name, known as the Rosary Priest! Many roadside billboards proclaimed one of his sayings, "The family that prays together, stays together."

Fr. Peyton's success baffled politicians and corporate executives. But his secret was really very simple: Prayer, especially the Rosary! If you want to read more about the very inspiring story of Fr. Peyton and the Rosary, I suggest reading his autobiography entitled *All For Her*.

SO, WHAT IS IT ABOUT PRAYER THAT IS SO POWERFUL?

Great saints have written volumes on this question. I can't add anything to that! But I do know that merely the act of "asking" is an act of humility. Asking implies we need help. We can't do it alone.

And most of us learn from our own day-to-day homework, projects and activities that often we won't receive help or understanding unless we ask for it.

Pride can prevent us from asking. We can be tempted to feel embarrassed if we have to ask for help. But that is just another trick of The Liar of liars! There's no shame in asking!

I mean, think of it, would you think less of a friend who asked for help? No way! You'd be glad to lend a hand if you knew they needed it!

In the same way - only bigger and more powerfully - God is always there to help us. And often He helps us through infusing the people we encounter with an eagerness and willingness to help us.

SO, WHAT DOES PRAYER INVOLVE?

I t's simple:

1. Asking God for guidance
2. Thanking in advance
3. Listening
4. Taking Action

Make these four steps a habit every day, and you'll be well on your way to knowing what God's purpose is for your life!

Of course, this needs to be something you will do the rest of your life to discover the ongoing beauty and joy God has in store for you along the way. You see, God reveals His plans to us day by day, every day. We just need to prepare ourselves through prayer, listening and observing, to recognize and receive those plans.

This was true even in the Old Testament. For example, in the first book of Samuel we read that the old prophet Eli helped young Samuel to respond to God's call. The advice was to listen:

> So the LORD called Samuel again for the third time. And he arose and went to Eli and said, "Here I am, for you called me." Then Eli discerned that the LORD was calling the boy.
>
> And Eli said to Samuel, "Go lie down, and it shall be if He calls you, that you shall say, 'Speak, LORD, for Your servant is listening.'" So Samuel went and lay down in his place.
>
> Then the LORD came and stood and called as at other times, "Samuel! Samuel!" And Samuel said, "Speak, for Your servant is listening."
>
> 1 Samuel 3:8-10

We too can strive daily to make Samuel's response our response: *Speak Lord, for Your servant is listening.*

AN IDEAL TEACHING AID FOR PRAYER

Most people are familiar with the Our Father prayer. This perfect **daily prayer for guidance** is what Jesus taught His disciples when they asked Him to "teach us to pray". (Luke 11:1-4).

> *Our Father,*
> *Who art in heaven,*
> *hallowed be Thy name;*
> *Thy kingdom come;*
> *Thy will be done on earth as it is in heaven.*
> *Give us this day our daily bread;*
> *and forgive us our trespasses*
> *as we forgive those who trespass against us;*
> *and lead us not into temptation,*
> *but deliver us from evil. Amen.*

One day I researched the full meaning of the Our Father prayer. As a result, I grew in appreciation for it and for the value of reciting it from the heart. Here are my reflections now when I pray the Our Father:

> *Our Father, (Abba/Daddy)*
> *Who art in heaven, (beauty beyond our comprehension)*
> *hallowed be Thy name; (holy is Your name)*
> *Thy kingdom come; (Your kingdom come in glory)*
> *Thy will be done on earth as it is in heaven.*
> *(Your ideal will in my life/our world)*
> *Give us this day our daily bread; (Your presence*
> *and Your word to feed on)*
> *and forgive us our trespasses (our selfishness,*
> *shortcomings or hurt we cause to others)*
> *as we forgive those who trespass against us;*
> *(others who hurt or offended us)*
> *and lead us not into temptation, (to do harm*
> *or evil to others or myself)*
> *but deliver us from evil. Amen. (Grant me grace*
> *and strength to do good. I believe.)*

When the Our Father is prayed this way it becomes a prayer from the heart and not just recited without our thinking.

St. Augustine and many other saints also reflected on this powerful prayer. You can get inspired by reading some of their writings on the Our Father prayer!

REMEMBER, an athlete cannot succeed without a good coach! You have the best coach there is – the one who hand-made you himself. God!

HOW DO I PRAY FOR GUIDANCE?

First and foremost remember that prayer is simply "conversation with God".

Some have asked me: "So how do I begin to ask for help? Where do I start? How do I listen to guidance from God?"

As the Nike brand advertisement promotes: "Just do it!"
That's right, just jump right in with both feet – don't look back – and just pray!

Here are some tips to help you feel more comfortable with developing the habit of prayer, but keep in mind – if you only read about it and don't jump in and do it every day, well…you can imagine the outcome of an athlete who only talked about swimming, but never got in the water. So, jump in!

YOUR TURN /

Following are a few tips that have helped me and others to get better at prayer:

1. Be still. Breathe, and quiet your mind and thoughts.

2. You might begin by closing your eyes and simply saying: "Lord God, I put myself in Your presence..."

3. Talk to Him just as you would talk with a good friend, from the heart.

4. Tell Him of your joys and sorrows or concerns.

Next, when you feel ready, any of these approaches can help you receive guidance after first putting yourself in God's great listening and loving presence:

Express simple Gratitude/Thanks/Appreciation for your many gifts and blessings, or for others, or even for the most difficult people and challenges in your life! Sometimes a prayer can be thanking God for all the annoying people and circumstances of your day. As odd as this sounds, it is a powerful way to pray because it puts the annoyances at Our Lord's feet and off our shoulders! He is so eager to help us bear our burdens that He welcomes our burdens with open arms!

Praise/Worship/Lift up for creation, beauty, nature, life and more.

Petition/Ask for help for others first, self second.

Forgive by reflecting, praying for a person/people who may have offended you.

Slowly read Scripture and think about what you read.

Contemplate/Be still/Be interiorly quiet (Listen).

In addition to the above methods, the following powerful, proven, effective prayers will help you greatly:

Mass. Attend (Pray) the most powerful of all prayers, the Holy Mass, on Sundays and, if possible, sometimes during the week too! God asks us to Keep Holy the Lord's Day, and our Faith teaches that there is nothing holier than to pray the Mass on Sunday - Our Lord's own sacrifice re-enacted in an unbloody manner, including His utter abandonment to and for us in the Eucharist. So, make attending Mass your Number One priority.

Rosary. Pray the Holy Rosary, the most powerful prayer after the Holy Mass. Read St. Louis de Montfort's Secrets of the Rosary and you'll get a taste of some of the awesome results of praying the Rosary. You'll also learn about the Rosary itself, its purpose and mysteries. Many other saints have written on the Rosary as well.

St. Dominic, for example, would pray the Rosary before every Mass he said. Often, the saint said, Mary would inspire him not to use the sermon he had carefully prepared, but instead to allow her to, basically, put the words in his mouth as he preached.

He became known for his amazing and powerful preaching that would even convert hardened sinners! St. Dominic also prayed the Rosary during one of the crusades. He prayed to defeat a horrific heresy of his day, the Albigensian heresy.

The Feast of Our Lady of the Rosary, on October 7, was established by Pope V in thanksgiving for granting victory to the Christian navy in their resounding defeat against the aggressive and powerful Turkish Islam invaders who had been relentlessly attacking Europe in an effort to destroy Christianity! This is a very inspiring story to read about, known as The Battle of Lapanto, fought in 1571, off the coast of Portugal.

Prayers of Saints. Praying written prayers that saints, popes and others have taken the time to write down can be helpful. (See the last pages of this book for additional samples and reference links.)

Another way to find solid guidance is by prayerfully reflecting upon God's living word of Scripture, as it is interpreted and presented to us through the Sacred Tradition of the Church – preserved in the teaching Magisterium of the same church Christ founded, which historically dates all the way back to Christ Himself.

Whether or not you have ever cracked open the Bible before, it is ridiculous not to pick it up and allow yourself to be guided by the words God spoke through the prophets and the writers of the Old and New Testaments.

You might begin by thinking of these writings in the Bible as "love letters" to you – from God.

FOLLOW THE LEAD OF THE GREAT ONES

When asked which books inspired them the most in life, more than 50 of the Founding Fathers of the United States of America said that the Bible had most inspired them.

Think about that for a second. The Bible inspired more than 50 of the Founding Fathers of this great nation! I wonder how many other leaders of other countries have been inspired by the Bible or by the living teachings of Christ?

The Emperor Constantine, in the year 312, literally changed the course of his country and of history when he converted to Christianity – and the Bible wasn't even printed yet!

THE BOOK IS WORTH READING!

When I was growing up, I used to think of the Bible as a huge and impossible book to read. "Too big, too much trouble," I thought. But I later discovered that the Bible was actually a compilation of many smaller books (much easier to read), written by many different inspired writers who God used throughout the ages.

KEEPING IT SIMPLE...

Once you discover that the Bible is made of smaller books, then Holy Scriptures don't seem so overwhelming to read! For example, the Old Testament (the first half of the Bible) begins with a book titled Genesis, which means "the beginning". In Genesis it is recorded that man is made in God's marvelous image. The Old Testament continues with four other books: Exodus, Leviticus, Numbers and Deuteronomy.

See how easy that was? These first five books recount the story of the formation of the people of God and of God's merciful relationship with man.

Now you are getting good at this! Let's keep going.

Another book in the Bible is the Psalms, which praise God's goodness and mercy even in the midst of great earthly sufferings. Even though these writings are from thousands of years before we were born, they still apply to you and me today! The Psalms are attributed to the writing of King David, the former shepherd boy who, as a young teenager, defeated the giant warrior Goliath with a slingshot. (Talk about trusting God!)

Then there are the books written by the great Old Testament prophets such as Isaiah and Jeremiah, foretelling the arrival of God's living Word in Jesus Christ.

The last book of the Old Testament, Macabees, includes an inspirational, stirring account of the brave man Judas Macabee,

who stood up to his people's oppressors with unrivaled courage and faith in the Lord. A friend of mine was so inspired by this one book alone in the Bible that she encouraged her Sixth Grade catechism class to name a sports team "The Macabees" to inspire fearless courage in the face of great obstacles! You just might think the same thing when you read this book of the Old Testament!

THE NEW TESTAMENT

M any of us are more familiar with the books of the New Testament (the books of the Bible that were written after Christ was born).

Of course the most famous of these New Testament books are the Four Gospels The word "Gospel" means "Good News", so these four books are four accounts written by four different authors telling of the "Good News" of Christ's existence. Indeed, Christ is the ultimate Good News because He alone is our salvation.

These four Gospels are the first four books in the New Testament and they tell of Christ's life, words and actions, giving first-hand, eye-witness historical accounts. The New Testament also includes the live-drama and historical documentation, letters, sufferings and discussions of the early church and its members. Again, every word is applicable to us today!

Once I understood that the Bible was just several smaller books put together into one big book and divided into two main parts, the Old Testament (before Christ was born) and the New Testament (after Christ was born), and that the Old Testament foreshadows Christ coming, then I was no longer intimidated by the Bible.

No more intimidation!
Now it was, and still is, exciting for me to pick up and learn from the Bible!

So, how can God tell you or guide you about things in your life through the reading of the passages in these holy writings?

Following the advice a wise priest shared with me, you might begin with the Gospel of St. John. John was the youngest of the apostles, and he lived the longest. He wrote the fourth book in the New Testament part of the Bible, the book called "The Gospel of John". Just as in other books of the New Testament, John gives an eye-witness, first-hand account of his time with Jesus.

Each of the four Gospels has what I call its own "flavor". St. John's Gospel seems to convey a flavor of Our Lord's love and mercy toward you and me. It is easy to begin with this book!

So, don't waste another minute. Get your hands on a Catholic Bible!

The Protestant versions of the Bible are OK, but they leave out a few wonderful books that were approved by the Church and handed down to us through the ages long before the 14th century printing press existed.

THE CATHOLIC CHURCH EXISTED LONG BEFORE THERE WERE PRINTING PRESSES!

You may not know this, but before the printing press was invented, Catholic monks would copy the entire Bible, word for word, by hand, in their beautiful, carefully executed handwriting. The monks did this for centuries! Year after year. As I mentioned earlier, there were no printing presses invented until the 14th century – that's more than 1,300 years after Christ walked the earth and founded His church!

So, I strongly encourage you to get a Catholic Bible. After all, you don't want to miss out on anything. My favorite printed version of the Bible is a Catholic version that shows all of Christ's words in red. But that's just a matter of taste.

After you get your Bible, then begin reading what the Apostle John wrote.

IT'S EASY TO READ A SHORT BOOK!

A priest in Michigan, Fr. Fortunata, often reminds students that the Gospel of John is only about 30 to 60 pages long, depending on the print size. Surely anyone can read a 30 to 60 page book!

How many books have you read that are only 30 or 60 pages long? That's an easy read for just about anyone! I sure am grateful now that I took that challenge and read it.

I was so inspired and grateful after reading the short Gospel of St. John, that I went on to read the Gospel of Matthew, then Mark, and finally Luke. I'm confident you can do it too! When you read these four books of the New Testament, I am certain that you'll be amazed by how much you will learn, gain and be inspired as well!

YOUR TURN /

Make a commitment! Even if you read only one page per day, for 30 to 60 days, you will have one of the four Gospels read in no time, and you will be all the better for it as well.

Q: What do you get when you read the Gospels?

A: Inspired! Compelled to do good. Enthusiasm!

And so much more of the good guidance we all need.

REFLECTION QUESTIONS FOR GUIDANCE

— Lord, what do You want me to do with my life?

— How can I best serve You and other people?

— Here I am Lord. I come to do Your will...
how do You want to use me?

A PRAYER
FOR GUIDANCE CLARITY

*Lord Jesus Christ, help me to live up to
whatever You want of me,
and to do so with generosity and joy.*

*Please help me to rest in the knowledge
that nothing is so worthwhile as
the fulfillment of my proper vocation.*

*Show me what You want me to do,
then give me the strength
and the courage to do it well.*

Amen.

ADDITIONAL REFLECTION
FOR GUIDANCE

*Trust in the Lord with all your heart;
and lean not unto thine own understanding.*

*In all your ways acknowledge Him,
and He shall direct thy paths.*

Proverbs 3: 5, 6

SIMPLE DAILY LIVING

First we have our daily duties,
those things "required" to be done.

Second come the present moments,
for us to "experience" one by one.

Third, we have
our hopes and dreams,
noble "promptings" that inspire...

These last are "callings" we must pursue
if we're to fulfill our heart's desire.

Joseph M. Tabers, © 2001

ONE MORE OF MY FAVORITE PRAYERS FOR GUIDANCE

THE POWERFUL SUSCIPE PRAYER
OF THE GREAT ST. IGNATIUS OF LOYOLA

Take Lord, and receive all my liberty,
my memory, my understanding,
and my entire will,
all that I have and possess.
Thou hast given all to me.
To Thee, O lord, I return it.
All is Thine, dispose of it wholly
according to Thy will.
Give me Thy love and Thy grace,
for this is sufficient for me.

To close this chapter on seeking God's guidance and His will, I share the following poem with you. It's something I was inspired to write a few years ago.

THE HAPPINESS/SUCCESS SECRET

*If you were to research all the ways for someone to be a success
and you were to list out all the steps it takes to find happiness,*

*Sooner or later you would find what others have discovered too...
just having the steps or formulas doesn't make it come to you.*

*You acknowledge most good things require planning, work and perspiration,
plus there is often sacrifice when dealing with a problem or frustration.*

*"It's the journey not the destination" yes, you've heard that said before,
but something else seems missing, you know there must be more.*

*So you begin to search for some kind of cause-effect relations
in the people that are happy; or sad with their situations.*

*You soon discover that the happiest seem to make the best of every day
and you notice a lot of gratitude in what they do and say.*

*But you keep a healthy skepticism saying, I'll believe more when I see it.
As you watch for some kind of proof, like a lightning bolt to hit.*

*Yet no flashes or miracles seem to instantly appear...
and still you're drawn to something, when the happiest are near.*

*It seems they're seeking for God's will, on ways they best can serve...
and not for selfish reasons or for what they might deserve.*

*When you notice this, you listen more and become more observant.
Even prayer changes to simply "Lord, help me to be a better servant."*

*So in the future if you're asked for the secret,
that makes our dreams come true?
Just say "you'll find success and happiness,
when you ask God's will for you".*

Joseph M. Tabers © November 2001

SUMMARIZING THE TAKEAWAYS

S o, in a nutshell: How do I ask and listen for God's guidance?

REMEMBER:

✓ **Listen always!** Pay attention to the little "promptings" of the Holy Spirit that God places in your heart, promptings to act selflessly for the good of others.

✓ **Appreciate the writings of Scripture.** Remember the word of God is spirit and life, and we all need both.

✓ St. Jerome, who lived in the year 420, once wrote: **"Ignorance of Scripture is ignorance of Christ."**

CHAPTER 3 ACTION TIPS:

○ **Talk with God every day.** If you are not already doing so... Begin now to get into the daily habit of Talking with God

○ **Ask God what His will is for you every day.** Begin now to get into the daily habit of asking God what His will is for you today.

○ **Be receptive and open.** Work at being receptive and open to the little signs He gives you in the people you encounter within the events of the day.

○ **Read a page a day.** Begin now to make a commitment to yourself to read at least one page per day from the Holy Scriptures (the Bible).

Chapter Four

CAPTURE DREAMS,GOALS AND SPIRITUAL PROMPTINGS IN WRITING:
Look for Clues

Vision – It reaches beyond the thing that is, into the conception of what can be. Imagination gives you the picture. Vision gives you the impulse to make the picture your own.

Robert Collier

Man is a goal-seeking animal. His life only has meaning if he is reaching out and striving for his goals.

Aristotle (384–322 BC)
Greek philosopher, studied under
Plato, tutored Alexander the Great

I've learned that the great challenge of life is to decide what's important and to disregard everything else.

Anonymous

Dream lofty dreams, and as you dream, so shall you become.

James Allen (1864–1912)
American author of the book, *As A Man Thinketh*

FIGURE IT OUT FOR YOURSELF

Figure it out for yourself, my lad,
You've all that the greatest of men have had;
Two arms, two hands, two legs, two eyes,
And a brain to use if you would be wise,
With this equipment they all began –
So start from the top and say, I CAN.

Look them over, the wise and the great,
They take their food from a common plate,
And similar knives and forks they use,
With similar laces they tie their shoes;
The world considers them brave and smart,
But you've all they had when they made their start.

You can triumph and come to skill,
You can be great if you only will;
You're well equipped for what fight you choose,
You have arms and legs and a brain to use;
And the man who has risen great deeds to do
Began his life with no more than you.

You are the handicap you must face,
You are the one who must choose your place.
You must say where you want to go,
How much you will study the truth to know;
God has equipped you for life, but He
Lets you decide what you want to be.

Courage must come from the soul within
The man must furnish the will to win.
So figure it out for yourself my lad,
You were born with all that the great have had;
With your equipment they all began,
Get hold of yourself and say, 'I CAN.'

George Washington Carver

When I started researching and reading more about the value and power of goal-setting, I was amazed to discover that when we put our dreams, goals and ideas into writing, we are at least 10 times more likely to accomplish them or make progress toward them. Ten times more likely! That's a lot!

I once read that the inventor Thomas Edison had a piece of paper and pencil in every room in his house. He believed that if you had a good idea, you better capture it right then and there, because if not, you might lose it for good!

MY RED STINGRAY BIKE

At the age of 10 or 11, I wanted a sharp-looking, red StingRay bike with a banana seat. I wanted that bike more than anything else in the world! But as the second youngest of six kids, my parents couldn't afford to just buy me a new bike. Instead, they taught me a great lesson in self-determination and encouraged me to start saving for my dream bike.

That seemed like a long, slow process to me. But I started saving anyway. I did odd jobs around our neighborhood. I shoveled snow during winter, washed cars and mowed lawns in the summer. Finally, after much oohing and aahing over department store sales

papers with pictures of bikes (and with a few dollars kicked in from Mom and Dad), I did get my dream bike.

That red StingRay bike meant a lot to me!

And even more so, because I had dreamed about, saved and worked hard for it.

Think about it...Anytime we work hard and sacrifice for something worth while, we appreciate it so much more.

Saving for that bike was a great life lesson for me. I learned valuable skills in persistence and work ethic that would serve me very well in future goal-planning.

I also learned that when you work toward, and succeed in achieving, a meaningful goal (in my case, personal transportation for an 11-year-old boy), you inspire confidence in your God-given abilities to do the even greater things He has planned for you.

WRITE IT DOWN: IMPROVE RESULTS!

It was not until later on, when I was 17 years old, that I read about the value and power of putting your goals down on paper, in writing, with a deadline. It seemed like a good idea to me. So one summer afternoon, on my parents' back porch, I began writing dreams and possible goals; things I would like to see come to life in the future. And you know what? Yes, it's true, many of those dreams and goals I wrote down years ago have·come to pass!

I could spend a lot of time here sharing with you true stories of my own written goals that have transpired (and I will share a few) but, the most important thing to remember is that God places desires in each of our hearts. In your heart and in the hearts of your friends, relatives, neighbors and acquaintances - are different dreams, hopes, and visions for the future. All of these can excite, fulfill, and compel you to take action for a greater good.

When you don't take the time to write these down, they can fade from your mind forever! So with that in mind, let's get focused and excited. Grab some paper (a simple or beautiful notebook would be even better) and a pen – Don't put it off!

Dreams and goals can inspire us to become co-creators with God in a sense. We can choose to use the gifts, abilities and experiences He's given us to make a positive difference in the world. In the next few pages, you will learn a proven-successful format for setting, following through on, and achieving worthwhile, meaningful goals.

YOUR TURN /

GETTING STARTED WITH GOAL-SETTING THAT WORKS

Let's start first with an easy to remember definition of goals. Goals are **specific, action-oriented targets** that can be visualized and committed to in writing. In other words, a "wish" is not a "goal".

A wish, however, can be converted to a goal when it has a plan, action steps and specific target dates.

HOW TO SET YOUR GOALS:

1. **Examine** your values and highest priorities. What is most important to you?

2. **Decide** on things you would like to **DO, HAVE, BE** or **BECOME.**

3. **Create** a clear **MENTAL** picture of the goal exactly as you would like to see it. Include as many **DETAILS** as possible.

4. **Write** these goals down on paper, then **DECIDE** by what month and year you believe you could realistically make it <u>happen</u>.

5. **Read** and **review** your goals often, especially early morning and late evening.

6. **Picture** yourself achieving these goals and vividly imagine what it feels like after you have achieved them.

PROGRESSIVE REALIZATION OF MEANINGFUL GOALS = SUCCESS

Notice that the definition of success in the subtitle above uses the words "meaningful goals", not just any goals.

One good way to determine if goals are meaningful and healthy for your future and your peace of mind is to ask yourself this question: "Will working on or achieving this goal draw me closer in relationship with God or further away from Him?"

No goal in the world is worth losing your soul or your relationship with God. Most meaningful goals have what I call the "greater good" factor. A goal is most likely to be more meaningful when it doesn't violate the laws of God or man and when it is genuinely for the greater good of other people.

THE VALUE OF WRITING (NOT JUST THINKING) YOUR GOALS

So...why bother putting goals, dreams and values in writing?

1. Writing down your goals helps you to see the big picture over a period of time, thereby reducing stress and fear of the unknown.

2. Visibility helps keep your attention focused on your highest priorities...otherwise, you know the old saying: "out of sight, out of mind".

3. Surprises can be evaluated and responded to more quickly when they can be immediately and easily compared to what you originally intended.

4. Interruptions and other demands are easier to decline or negotiate when your plans and priorities are in writing and in front of you at all times.

5. Recovery time or "getting back on track" is easier when you have something in writing to which you can refer.

6. Writing things down helps to clarify our thinking and creates more commitment to actually doing it.

WHAT EFFECTIVE GOAL-SETTING LOOKS LIKE:

1. Write a realistic **Goal (Vision) for the future.**

2. Develop a specific **Plan (Steps)** for achieving the goal.

3. Do **(Act on)** one of the specific steps in the plan.

4. **Adjust** the plan as needed to adapt to change, or to reflect adjustments made to your vision, progress or new realities that may affect your goal as it was originally written.

Repeat Steps 1-4. This proven goal-setting process gets results! It will work for you and for anyone who uses it.

One word of caution: Before using this process, make sure that your goals are well-rounded and anchored in noble values.

History has proven over and over again that self-centered goals or lopsided goals (having too many goals in one category/area, such as having too many financial goals and not enough spiritual or physical goals) often leads to self-destruction or harm to others. So, to avoid the trap of lopsided goals, let's take some time now to reflect on some of your lifetime goals in multiple categories.

GOAL CATEGORIES THAT MAKE LIFE MEANINGFUL
SOME OF MY LIFETIME GOALS

Sadly, it is estimated that only about one in 20 people actually take the time to write down their goals. If you are one of the fortunate "one in 20" who already has his or her goals in writing, then the following exercise will be a great review and refresher. If this is the first time you are writing down your goals, it may be one of the most valuable uses of your time right now because written goals can have a positive impact on your life for years to come.

YOUR TURN /

Directions: Take a few minutes right now to write at least one specific thing you would like to achieve in each of the following areas of your Life:

- SPIRITUAL (prayer, reading, retreats) I will:

- FAMILY (relationships, planning, caring, sharing) I will:

- SOCIAL (personal activities, hobbies, friendships) I will:

- COMMUNITY (contribution, giving back, building, service to others) I will:

- PERSONAL/SELF-DEVELOPMENT (education, reading, goal-setting, health) I will:

- FINANCIAL (net worth, savings or debt reduction) I will:

Congratulations! By writing at least one goal for each of the six areas above you just increased the odds tremendously that you will make progress toward these goals and be more excited about doing so in the process. Later on we will help you prioritize and add specific details to one of these goals to help accelerate its accomplishment.

Like spokes in a wagon wheel, when we have goals for the most important aspects of human existence, then our lives are more likely to have a sense of balance.

One thing I've noticed as a weakness of many goal-setting programs is that they often don't address the purpose, or the "why" for the goal(s).

I believe that a clear purpose or "why" for a goal is what keeps us motivated to stick with it. So, next, we'll take a look at the importance of examining the underlying principles that drive your goals. That means making sure your goals are in harmony with healthy, life-giving principles.

WHAT PRINCIPLES ARE DRIVING (OR UNDERLYING) MY GOALS AND PRIORITIES IN LIFE?

Take one minute right now and quickly write down the three things that are most important to you in life as of right now. Don't over-analyze here...just write them down:

> ### The Three Things I Value Most in Life as of Right Now are:
>
> 1.
> 2.
> 3.

Once you have done this exercise, it will give you a snapshot into what I have come to call "get out of bed motivation". In order to stay motivated, your goals should support at least two of the three things you value most in life.

For example, my original list had:

1. Serve God
2. Help people
3. Be a better person

By the way, you may be interested to know that whenever I ask live audiences, "By a show of hands, how many of you included family as one of your three most important?" consistently almost every hand goes up!

WHY THE <u>REASONS</u> FOR YOUR GOALS ARE SO IMPORTANT: WHAT IS PRINCIPLE-BASED GOAL SETTING?

The Number One reason why people **don't** achieve greater success with their goals is that they'd rather experience comfort or complacency instead of sacrifice and effort. It is the same reason why people don't achieve greater success in other areas of their life such as eating right and exercising.

Think about it. What are you willing to give in return for progress on worthwhile goals? Are you willing to sacrifice some of your time, energy, effort or money?

And don't kid yourself. You'll certainly be faced with obstacles as soon as you set your mind to achieving your written goals. Many of those obstacles will be self-imposed, in spite of your best intentions. As long as you are aware of this, you can avoid the pitfalls.

For example, take Procrastination – you know, it's that little voice inside your head that tells you "oh, do it tomorrow", "later", or "I don't feel like it today". Procrastination can affect us in all areas of life if we don't stay focused and disciplined.

One of the best ways to overcome procrastination is to make sure your meaningful goals are based on noble, worthwhile principles and priorities. This will help pull you through when the going gets rough. Making sure your goals support and are consistent with your core principles and priorities will allow you to say "no" to distractions or excuses in order to help you stay on track and say "yes" to a better future.

WE ALL NEED A PURPOSE AND A ROADMAP FOR THE JOURNEY

Imagine taking a long-distance trip to a foreign land, but not having any reason to go there. Silly, isn't it? Yet we often do this with our work and even with our future plans.

Sitting down and thinking through not only <u>what</u> is most important but <u>why it is most important</u> requires effort, soul searching and sometimes discomfort…maybe that is why more people don't take time to do it.

But reading and working through this book, you will not be like most people! Instead, you will begin to have a clear sense of passion and purpose for your life, at any age!

On the following few pages is an easy-to-use, value-prioritizing exercise designed to help you overcome procrastination and to increase the amount of peace of mind and contentment you experience while working toward your goals.

Once you complete this exercise, I believe you will find that it's a great way to expand your thinking, clarify things you were not sure of and discover ways to begin or continue with renewed enthusiasm toward at least one of your written goals.

Fueling Your Vision
for The Future
Prioritize
What's Important
to You

Circle five or six priorities that you believe are important for you to succeed with your goals. Next, prioritize the top three core principles (of those circled) that you believe will best support your vision for your preferred future. Write these Top Three on a 3 x 5 card.

adventure	excellence	humor
collaboration	excitement	initiative
commitment	fairness	innovation
community support	faith	integrity
competition	financial growth	justice
continuous-	flexibility	learning
improvement	freedom	leaving a legacy
control	fulfillment	love
cooperation	fun	loyalty
courage	happiness	making a difference
creativity	hard work	obedience
dependability	honesty	order
efficiency	honor	originality

peace	respect	stewardship
persistence	responsiveness	success
perspective	sacrifice	support for others
profitability	security	teamwork
positive attitude	self-control	trust
purposefulness	service to other	truth
quality	sincerity	variety
recognition	spirituality	wisdom
relationships	stability	

Others:_____

> *A humble knowledge of thyself is a surer way to God than a deep search after learning.*
>
> Thomas á Kempis (1380–1471)
> German monk, devotional author

At this point, you should have your goal categories completed, with one goal in each of the six categories mentioned earlier in this chapter on page 73. Now you have a great opportunity to accelerate your progress by detailing at least one of your goals on the following Goal Contract worksheet.

The Goal Contract worksheet is the same goal worksheet that I have personally used, and helped others use, to make progress on and eventually complete several of our own goals successfully. I don't know about you, but I sure like proven formats that actually work...and it is for this reason that I am confident this written format will work for you too!

Goal Contract
A helpful goal-achieving worksheet
(Below is one of my first written and completed goals... These forms really work!)

Goal Area: __Financial__ Core Principles: __Business development, helping people/service__

TARGET DATE AND SPECIFIC GOAL (written as if already achieved)

It is _____November 31, 1978_____ and I ___Joe Tabers___ have:
　　　　　　(month, day, year)

Saved $3,500 for 15% down payment on the purchase of my first two-family income property.

I feel... Excited and proud that I followed through. This first property has increased
　　　　(describe emotions)
　　　my real estate skills and my self-confidence.

EXPECTED BENEFITS - REACHING THIS GOAL WILL BENEFIT
ME/OTHERS IN THE FOLLOWING WAYS:

This savings will allow me to begin investing in real estate and help my savings to grow faster and give others a nice place to live.

I AM WILLING TO GIVE OF THE FOLLOWING IN EXCHANGE
FOR ACHIEVING THIS GOAL (TIME, MONEY ETC.):

Being frugal for the next six months. Sticking strictly to an "essentials only" spending plan. Working as much overtime and side jobs as possible.

OBSTACLES/ROADBLOCKS - THINGS THAT STAND BETWEEN ME
AND MY ACHIEVING THIS GOAL:

Lack of self-discipline, unnecessary purchases, emergency car repairs.

SOLUTIONS/PLANS - I WILL OVERCOME THESE OBSTACLES
BY TAKING THESE SPECIFIC STEPS:
- Keeping focused on making steady progress
- Avoiding shopping and impulse purchases
- Keeping my car maintained well to avoid repairs

I WILL MEASURE PROGRESS ONLY BY COMPLETING DO-ABLE SMALLER
TASKS THAT LEAD TO GOAL ACCOMPLISHMENT AS FOLLOWS:

	Date:	Action or Measurable Benchmark:
Task 1	6/30/78	Have first $600 deposited in credit union
Task 2	7/31/78	Second $600 deposited $1,200 total
Task 3	8/30/78	Third $600 deposited $1,800 total
Task 4	10/30/78	Have $1,200 more deposited $3,000 total

Only $500 more to save by 11/31/78
Goal Partner (supportive person): Dorthy Warner (aunt), Jane Taberski (sister)

YOUR TURN /

Goal Contract   Helpful Goal-Achieving Worksheet

Goal Area: _____ Core Principles: _____

TARGET DATE AND SPECIFIC GOAL (written as if already achieved)
It is _____ and I _____ have:
     (month, day, year)

_____

I feel..._____
    (describe emotions)

EXPECTED BENEFITS - REACHING THIS GOAL WILL BENEFIT
ME/OTHERS IN THE FOLLOWING WAYS:

I AM WILLING TO GIVE OF THE FOLLOWING IN EXCHANGE
FOR ACHIEVING THIS GOAL (TIME, MONEY ETC.):

OBSTACLES/ROADBLOCKS - THINGS THAT STAND BETWEEN ME
AND MY ACHIEVING THIS GOAL:

SOLUTIONS/PLANS - I WILL OVERCOME THESE OBSTACLES
BY TAKING THESE SPECIFIC STEPS:

I WILL MEASURE PROGRESS ONLY BY COMPLETING DO-ABLE SMALLER
TASKS THAT LEAD TO GOAL ACCOMPLISHMENT AS FOLLOWS:

	Date:	Action or Measurable Benchmark:
Task 1	_____	_____
Task 2	_____	_____
Task 3	_____	_____
Task 4	_____	_____

Goal Partner (supportive person): _____

HAVE A PLAN

Have a plan.

Have a plan!

Hey, young woman,

hey, young man.

Just sit down with a pen in hand,

then decide and take a stand.

Reflect on things you're being called to do,

write them down then prioritize too.

You'll find time for almost everything,

during summer, winter, fall and spring.

Yes, time is the same for everyone,

so plan yours out, it can be fun.

It's not that much for you to do

and you'll be glad you did it too.

Because step by step is the master key.

Yes one by one you soon will see

that many of the plans you feel called to do,

they'll go your way...

Dreams can come true.

Joseph M. Tabers

SUMMARIZING THE TAKEAWAYS

So, in a nutshell: How do I capture dreams, goals and clues from God in writing?

REMEMBER:

✓ "BE" or "BEcome" character goals are always more important than the "Do" or "Have" goals.

✓ Use the six categories of goals to make sure your use of time is well-rounded and balanced with your priorities.

✓ Make sure your written goals are congruent with your three highest principles.

✓ Goals that benefit other people always bring us the greatest long term happiness and excitement.

CHAPTER 4 ACTION TIPS:

○ **Write it down!** Sit down and write out all the things you feel called to do, whether they are dreams or goals.

○ **Carry your Top Three.** Reflect on the three things most important to you in life. Write these Top Three on a 3 x 5 card to carry in your wallet or purse.

○ **Review Daily.** For self-motivation, regularly read and review your values and highest principles.

○ **Take One Step at a Time.** Focus on completing one or two action steps on one of your written goals-make some progress each day or each week!

○ **Choose simply and humbly,** to live by values and goals that give glory to God.

Chapter Five

SHARE YOUR HOPES WITH SUPPORTIVE PEOPLE: Help from Others Helps

Hope is the confident expectation of fulfillment.

*Hope is a **belief** in a positive outcome related to events and **circumstances** in one's life.*

Webster's dictionary

A vision without a task is but a dream, a task without a vision is drudgery, a vision and a task is the hope of the world.

Written on a wall in a Church in Sussex, England circa 1730

The greatest architect and the one most needed is hope.

Henry Ward Beecher, (1813 - 1887)

I n addition to having written goals and plans, try sharing your important goals with those whom you believe will be encouraging, supportive, or helpful. Some people mistakenly think that they can or should "go it alone". While there may be periods of time when this is required of us, we are usually at our best when serving, working with or interacting with others.

All of us need or at least appreciate encouragement at times. Later on in Chapter 8, I'll address how important it is for us to encourage others, and we'll explore some ways we can do that.

FOR NOW, LET'S LOOK AT RELATIONSHIP SUPPORT AND THE POWER OF ENCOURAGEMENT!

F irst, it is wise for us to trust that God is our **biggest** fan and cheerleader. Never lose sight of that truth. After all, He created us exactly as we are and He wants what is best for us more than anyone else ever could want it. God wants – and knows – what is best for us even more than we know it or want it ourselves!

"For I know the plans I have for you," declares the LORD, *"plans to prosper you and not to harm you, plans to give you hope and a future."* (Jeremiah 29:11)

S econd, for most of us, our parents and family members are usually our **next biggest** source of encouragement and support, followed by our friends with whom we choose to surround ourselves.

Assuming that you know at least one person whom you respect and admire (maybe someone from your list in Chapter 1), don't be afraid to ask for that person's help and verbal support. Asking for, and accepting, help from others is a healthy thing for us to do. (unless, of course, we expect that person to do all the work for us! That wouldn't be right.)

Unfortunately in our society today, as I mentioned in an earlier chapter, asking for help has become wrongly perceived as a sign of weakness. But in reality, most wise leaders past and present have done just that on a regular basis! They've asked for help. Asking for help, and allowing others to help us, is an act of humility. It makes us aware that we need each other, that we can't do it alone.

Just as a business needs customers to grow and profit, and just as an athlete needs a coach in order to perform better, so too we accelerate our progress with a little help from a friend, business associate, coach or family member.

GOOD LUCK, JOE!

One of my early experiences of the power that comes from receiving support from others was when I shared my written goal to purchase a piece of real estate while I was still a teenager. You saw my original real estate goal written out in the previous chapter. That was a big goal for someone my age! And anyone could have easily laughed at my goal. I realized this, but I also learned and understood the value of sharing a goal with a trusted friend or family member for additional accountability or motivation.

You see, at the time I had read about the value and power of having specific written goals - the same principles that I shared with you in Chapter 4. I also had read about the importance of having a witness to your goals. And I mean a real, true, fully engaged witness. So with this in mind, I thought about with whom I would share my real estate goal. I selected my optimistic, entrepreneurial-type hair stylist sister, Jane, along with my supportive aunt, Dorothy. They both signed my written goal statement with the verbal encouragement, "Good Luck, Joe!"

Even though Jane and Aunt Dorothy might have held inside a little healthy skepticism about my ability to achieve that goal, they didn't tell me about their inner doubts. Nope. They just appeared to be rooting for me, 200%! Now I felt like I had two people "in my corner!" It made me more confident and determined to achieve my goal. Somehow, I knew I could do it now.

And you know what? It worked! I did it!

About 18 months later, just two weeks before my 20th birthday, at the age of only 19, I stepped into my first (of eventually four) investment properties by age 23. To this day, I can still see it: A brick two-family bungalow that I cleaned, fixed-up and rented to two separate tenants.

Imagine the thrill of achieving that goal! And, Boy, did that ever boost my confidence and convictions about the importance of both written goals and enlisting the support of others!

Whether the purpose of our support "team" is merely for accountability and to remind us of our commitments so that we do not give up too easily, or whether it is because it makes us feel like we have to achieve the goal so as not to let others down, it doesn't matter. It works!

GETTING ENCOURAGEMENT FROM A CLUB OR GROUP

A few years later, I recall another experience of encouragement and support that shaped my future and my calling.

After sharing with others my dream of speaking and teaching large audiences useful information to help them improve their lives, a business colleague told me about an organization called Toastmasters International. I had never heard of Toastmasters before, but she assured me it would help improve my listening, thinking and speaking skills. I was excited to learn that Toastmasters had local clubs in major cities throughout the U.S. and beyond, so I looked up a local club and attended their weekly meetings.

Well, Toastmasters exposed me (at the age of 21) to a terrific group of people who wanted the best for each of their fellow club members. It was great fun and a great learning experience!

And yes, it was in large part because of the encouragement, example and feedback from my local Toastmasters group that I got bit by the "speaking bug". It was at that time a passion grew in me for public speaking and working with audiences.

Within two years, at the age of 23, I received one of my first paid speaking opportunities, namely to speak to a local high school for a grand total of $50 and a hot lunch.

It would be another two years of hard work, persistence and words of encouragement from peers before I could earn enough from professional speaking to go into it as my full-time vocation and profession.

Throughout this time (ages 18 to 25), the written words and encouragement of other generous book authors, speakers, and leaders as well as their audio-recordings were my constant support. I learned from reading the writings of achievement authors such as Maxwell Maltz, Napoleon Hill and Dale Carnegie. And I learned from reading and hearing the writings of authors of faith from the New Testament to Mother Teresa, Pope John Paul II, Thomas Kempis, and many others.

```
Never underestimate
    the power of reading a helpful,
    well-written book

or listening to a well-planned,
    inspiring speech...

either of these can change your
life for the better!

Never underestimate the power of
enlisting committed encouragers!

WE ALL NEED INSPIRATION.
```

BUT WHO CAN I TRUST, AND HOW?

Today more than ever I am convinced that we can, and should, learn from others who have gone before us. None of us stands alone. Even as a culture, as a society, as a country and community, we stand on the shoulders of the great, inspiring men and women who have gone before us throughout history, especially those who have been officially declared to be saints by the Church. None of them did it alone!

Like those who inspired others before us, you too can benefit from surrounding yourself with selfless people who really want what is best for you, just as you should want the best for them! In fact, it reminds me of one of the best definitions of love I have ever read. It went something like this: **Real love is to simply and truly want what is best for another human being.**

You will be able to spot and recognize these people, and you will be able to recognize whether they are genuine or not, because the genuine individuals are not focused on getting something for themselves. They aren't seeking anything from you in return, other than to see you do well.

Think about that. Who do you know like this? Do you belong to any groups whose members are supportive, encouraging people who want you to be your best?

YOUR TURN /

Start now, if you haven't already done so, and take the time to check out some of the great organizations in your local area which have very generous members who are eager to share and encourage you in achieving your noble goals.

Following is a list of just a few of the many groups and types of organizations that may fit your personality and style. Tip: when you visit an organization, look for ways you can contribute. All organizations need volunteers and you will grow faster and build stronger relationships when you are contributing.

- Small, faith-based groups – such as a men's, women's or young adult group that meets regularly at a local parish.

- Toastmasters International – for improving listening, thinking and speaking skills, with clubs in most geographical areas.

- Knights of Columbus – a terrific and active men's group dedicated to serving others with impressive, faith-filled service projects, and that has "councils" in many local parishes.

- Lions Clubs – which support a number of projects such as help for the blind.

- Kiwanis clubs – improves the quality of Life for Children and Families.

- Worldwide Catholic business clubs – which are springing up in many cities across the country.

- Online resources can also help you find local groups, or even online social networking groups, although in my opinion nothing can take the place of real-live-person-to-person interaction and encouragement! These online resources include the Catholic Business Journal (www.CatholicBusinessJournal.biz), which lists local Catholic business clubs in your area, and another website;

- www.MyDream.com, which is a diverse and creative website where people from around the world share their dreams, learn from others and stay accountable.

So what are you waiting for?!

You don't need a formal invitation! Just request some information from any club or organization that sounds interesting to you, or just show up as a guest at one of their meetings. You will be welcomed at the meeting, and can make a decision regarding whether or not this is the right group to start with once you've experienced the group firsthand at one or several meetings.

WHEN OTHERS YOU KNOW MAY BE CYNICAL

During some of the live workshops I conduct throughout the year, participants have asked me more than a few times; "what do you do when many of the people you know, whether they are co-workers, friends, or even family members, are often cynical or, even worse, downright negative whenever you share any positive plans or good news with them?"

My short answer is…get new friends!

While there may be some truth in that approach, my sincere answer is…*Why would you tell certain people your goals if you expect a cynical, negative response?*

There is an old truth in psychology that goes like this: *The best predictor of someone's future behavior is generally his or her past behavior.*

An exception to this rule would be if this person went through a significant emotional event or if he or she concretely and clearly demonstrated a consistent change in behavior, such as St. Paul, after getting knocked off his horse on his way from Jerusalem to Damascus. As you may remember in that incident, St. Paul was on his way to persecute the Christians and God knocked him off his horse, spoke audibly to him, asking "why do you persecute me?" and temporarily blinded him so that he was dependent on his fellow companions to lead him to the city. Clearly St. Paul's actions changed dramatically from persecuting Christians to living and leading Christians!

But even the Christians in Damascus did not at first trust Paul's new behavior. Talk about a man with a reputation! It was only after seeing a consistent and clear change of heart that the Christians knew they could trust Paul.

The same is true as you consider whether or not someone is worthy of being entrusted with your goals. Look for people who have a history of encouraging others in a selfless manner.

HOPE AND GOOD NEWS

Even if you do not have supportive or caring family members around you, there are still other ways you can get support.

You can begin building support for your dreams by reading helpful books, listening to inspiring audio recordings, and of course sharing your dreams and hopes with the Lord. Whenever you share your hopes and dreams with God, be sure to ask Him for guidance, to help you hear and follow His will in your life.

You can also do your part by making a short list of two or three people who are in a field or vocation of interest to you. Call or e-mail these people and offer to buy them lunch in exchange for a brief interview with them about their line of work. Most professionals will be happy to talk with you. Be sure to remember to respect their time.

WHY NOT JUST DO IT MYSELF?

We are designed by our Creator for social interaction. We need each other. Interaction with God and other people strengthens our own identity.

In time of war, it has been said that solitary confinement (for an extended length of time) is the most severe and tortuous form of

14 Ways to Be or Stay At Your Best

From the book **God Has GREAT Plans** for You!

- Choose to see the good in others.
- Practice the virtues you admire in others.
- Choose to be grateful... daily.
- Look for clues in the experiences, talents and gifts you've been blessed with.
- Ask God for guidance in all decisions.
- Write down goals/dreams –look for hints
- Ask for help from supportive people.
- Offer to help or assist someone in need without being asked.
- Do the most generous thing in front of you right now; even if it's inconvenient.
- Show concern for every soul.
- Be first to apologize in misunderstandings.
- Read scripture or spiritual writings daily.
- Pray, to do God's will daily.
- Share recognition/show appreciation for the talents and gifts of others.

For more information about the book visit:

© GodHasGreatPlans.com – 1-800-805-8780

God Has Great Plans for You! - Reviews

"This book is a gem in so many ways! For young people, for busy professionals, for everyone. This should be a classic tool for every Christian searching for peace in life." -Patrick Lencioni, bestselling business author, The Five Dysfunctions of a Team

"I REALLY LIKED IT! I have wanted a book like this for many years. We are always looking for some program which will guide a young man or woman in forward-looking reflection, yet based on true Catholic reality - that God is with us, and calls us to Him, each uniquely and wonderfully. Thank you Joe, for the gift of vocational guidance in a real, to-the-point, and personal "conversation" with our high school students. It will become a permanent part of our curriculum." -Michael Van Hecke, M.Ed. Headmaster, Saint Augustine Academy, Ventura, CA

"In a world our teens often find overwhelming and discouraging, this book offers a semesters worth of practical advice that every high school student should know and apply. I found the text easy to read and the chapter exercises with takeaways were also great teaching tools. There is much value for each person who reads this book." -Brian Wolcott, Principal, Fr. Gabriel Richard High School, Ann Arbor, MI

Read more at www.GodHasGreatPlans.com

Chapter Six

BLOOM WHERE YOU ARE PLANTED;
Do Good Now, Add Value!

Each one of you has received a special grace, so, like good stewards responsible for all these different graces of God, put yourselves at the service of others.

1 Peter 4:10

We make a living by what we get, but we make a life by what we give.

Winston Churchill

The greatest good you can do for another is not just to share your riches, but to reveal to him his own.

Benjamin Disraeli
British politician (1804 - 1881)

You have been told, O man, what is good, and what the LORD requires of you: Only to do the right and to love goodness, and to walk humbly with your God.

Micah 6:6-8

S trive now to do your present responsibilities (school or work) to the best of your abilities. Always seek to learn, improve, and work to do a job or task even better.

Serve well now, right were you are, in your current circumstances and current situation. **Add value now, right were you are**, in your present surroundings and existing relationships.

What I want to emphasize is: *Don't fight where God has you, right here, right now.* Embrace it! All work has meaning and value if we look for it. Yes, all work (even the most menial or routine) can be meaningful and prepare us to better handle God's future plans for us.

LOOK AROUND YOU, RIGHT NOW

A lot of individuals, young people included, look outside their current reality. They look at how others are doing and compare themselves to them. Even if you are a student and still in school, this applies to you too! Don't get caught up comparing yourself to others. Remind yourself that doing good and adding value is not a form of competition.

Instead, be the best you can be with where you are, and with what you are - whether you are in school as a student or a waitress/waiter in a restaurant; share your best. Don't waste precious time complaining and wishing you were somewhere else or doing something else.

Forget it! Complaining is not the path to success. This kind of thinking doesn't help anybody and will never lead you to discover God's great plans for your life! Never! It will only make you, and those around you, more tense and less happy with life.

ONE OF MY EARLIEST EXPERIENCES
OF "BLOOM WHERE YOUR PLANTED"

I was about 12 years old. It was a beautiful sunny morning. School was just out for summer vacation and I had just finished breakfast and was gazing out of the front living room window of our family home in Michigan.

My mother saw me from the kitchen and asked "what are you looking at?"

"I'm watching our elderly neighbor, Mr. Tifer, getting ready to mow his lawn," I replied.

Then mom challenged me with "why don't you go and help him?"

"No, that's okay" was my standard kid response.

Mom then insisted "go on...you're not doing anything anyway... go and make yourself useful!" I reluctantly agreed and sauntered over to see if I could help. At the time, Mr. Tifer was more that 80 years old, slightly bent over, and a bit frail. He had just started up his gas-powered mower and was pushing it slowly along when I arrived on his front walkway. He did not notice me at first.

So I looked around and spotted a star-wheeled, manual sidewalk lawn edger that Mr. Tifer had brought out to use later. I picked it up and began rolling along the edge of the sidewalk where the grass crept over, making a clean-cut edge with the tool.

Stopping only to help Mr. Tifer empty the grass catcher into a trash can from time to time, we were done in about 30 or 40 minutes, including sweeping up stray grass. As I was saying "goodbye" to head back home, the old man motioned for me to wait a minute as he reached into his pocket. He pulled out one of those rubber coin purses that you squeeze, and reached in for a few quarters...

My eyes followed the shiny coins with eager surprise as he began to hand them to me and then, all of a sudden, I blurted out "no thanks Mr. Tifer...I just wanted to help."

Then an interesting thing happened that would stay with me the rest of my life. As I turned and walked away, a feeling of accomplishment flooded over me and I ran into our house to tell my Mom.

I said "Mom, guess what? I just helped Mr. Tifer and he went to pay me... and I didn't accept it!" Mom reinforced my good feeling, responding "good for you! I'm proud of you." And, to be honest, I was proud of myself too. But more importantly, I learned first hand the incredible joy and internal satisfaction we get when we serve another without expecting anything in return. And that same joyful lesson still is with me to this day whenever I practice it. Just as it is with you, whenever you help someone unasked, without expecting anything in return.

From that day on something clicked for me. I came to realize that **the joy we get when we serve others without want of a reward is its own reward.** If you haven't experienced it before or even if it has been awhile since you have had that rewarding joy-filled feeling, now is the perfect time to practice an act of selfless service again.

YOUR TURN ✎

A GOOD WAY TO BEGIN

A sk yourself: Who is in need and who could use my help right now? What is it that they might need?

Then go do it! Write that note, send that card, make that long overdue phone call, or stop and make that unexpected visit. Offer a friend, neighbor, or your parents a helping hand on a project that they are working on. You'll be glad you did!

Always remember, whenever you help someone...not one, but **two** people end up feeling better.

A QUICK "ACID TEST" TO CHECK YOUR MOTIVES

Ask yourself:

- Am I doing this, or wanting to do this, in order to call attention to myself? (indicating pride and ego motives)

- Am I doing this truly to help one or more people, without want of attention or reward? (indicating selfless and other-focused motives)

Slowing down to honestly reflect on our motives can help us keep a healthy perspective.

BECOME OVER-QUALIFIED AND UNDER-PAID!

Here is one of the great secrets of life: **If you want a better job, then work at becoming so good that you get overqualified and underpaid for the job you're currently doing.** In other words, practice doing more than you are getting paid to do. Go the extra mile!

Think about it. Most people won't earn a better job if they view their current job with an attitude of "I'm not getting paid enough to do this work, so I'll just bide my time here until I find something better". No. The reality is that **we are forming habits this very minute that will affect us the rest of our life,** for better or worse. If we spend our time thinking about how a job isn't good enough for us, guess what. Our next job will not be good enough either, and so a downward cycle continues.

Yes, if you want a better job, then do the best you possibly can, right where you are, right now! Every CEO, leader or business owner I ever met, truly appreciates and rewards their employees who have this attitude and work ethic.

You know, sometimes we can get so focused on looking for the ideal job or work or club to get involved with that we end up missing opportunities that are right in front of us, all around us.

> *I long to accomplish a great and noble task, but it is my chief duty to accomplish humble tasks as though they were great and noble. The world is moved along, not only by the mighty shoves of its heroes, but also by the aggregate of the tiny pushes of each honest worker.*
>
> Helen Keller

DON'T LET "PERFECT" BE THE ENEMY OF "GOOD"

At some point in our lives, most of us dream of doing something great. We yearn to make a difference in the world, to help other people and to help make the world a better place. We might dream of heroically saving someone's life, or going on a foreign mission in some far away, exotic country to serve the needy.

One word of caution:

DON'T just sit and dream
about the ideal opportunity to serve.

Get up,
    look around you
    and serve where you are...

God has you where you are
    for a reason.

The good news is that you and I do not have to go very far to make a difference. Often the best place to start serving is with the people who are around us right now.

Our first and primary responsibility is to serve those closest to us, this often means our family, our friends, our co-workers and our neighbors and community. In other words, we do well when we bloom where we are planted!

Even Jesus tought us: *Give and more will be given to you* (Luke 6:38). So whenever we serve, learn, grow or improve ourselves, it enables us to give greater value to other people's lives.

REMINDERS FOR GOING THE EXTRA MILE

Trust that most other people do notice or at least appreciate when you go the extra mile to:

- Make sure a job is done right

- Make sure other people have their needs met or exceeded

- Make sure you show that you care

- Make sure you put a little extra effort into a job

- Make sure that you double-check to ensure accuracy

I learned first-hand, and many times over, the value of extra effort and the opportunities that it can create. Here are a few quick examples.

- As a teenager owning my first rental property, I cleaned and prepared it so well that I was able to attract better quality tenants who were willing to appreciate and take care of the property and willing to pay slightly higher rent for a well-cared for property. It was a win-win situation.

- After only working three years in commercial building maintenance, I was offered a leadership position as the foreman because of my initiative and work ethic. That earned me an extra $1.25 per hour immediately, without ever asking for it.

- From working on cars and houses in my spare time and banking the extra income, I was able to take additional evening classes as well as subscribe to many audio CD courses that improved my skills.

Each and every time I learned more or grew more, it gave me more resources with which to better serve and help other people.

Anytime you or I grow or improve ourselves, no matter whether we improve our knowledge, skills or abilities, we automatically increase our service value to and for others. But there is one exception. All of these improvements would be useless unless we are willing to be happy to serve God and do all that He wants.

As Jean-Pierre de Caussade wrote, A well-disposed heart unites us with God's will. Without it, we behave according to our own natural impulses and usually fight against the divine plans. God, strictly speaking, uses only the humble as His instruments.

These poems are reminders for blooming wherever we are...

WORTHWHILE "INTERRUPTIONS"

We go to here
we go to there
as busy as can be.

The problem is
that when we rush
we sometimes fail to see;

The people God places in our path
are not there to make us tense.
They may be opportunities
for us to make a difference.

Notice when we do slow down
and give someone our best,
a small connection does take place
that puts our soul at rest.

Maybe it's just a sincere smile
or a warm or friendly greeting;
or even a little acknowledgment
when two stranger's eyes are meeting.

Sure, there are times when we don't plan
to invest much time in listening,
to someone sharing a little stress
or heartache with eyes a-glistening.

And yes it's true we have "things to do"
calling us to quit this attention giving;
but something inside reminds us,
of the value of each life that's living.

So the next time we encounter
Someone in need passing by our way
and our busy schedule
is causing tension in our day...

Let's remember - just to slow down
even if the timing doesn't make good sense,
this "interruption" could be God calling us
to make a difference.

Joseph M. Tabers © 2001

EVERYDAY SUPERHEROES

We may not know, we may not see
supernatural heroes next to you and me.

Be it a thoughtful boss or one of our friends
or just someone who listens when we're frazzled at ends.

A helpful store clerk or courteous student
or a parent's kind words when the timing is prudent.

Just a little of their efforts can go a long way
to give us some hope or even brighten our day.

When in our struggles or stresses, or with illness bedridden,
we encounter one who cares…something divine is hidden.

The supernatural exists in ordinary events of each day
in the problems and the joys we meet along our way.

Oh yes there are heroes just take a look around
it doesn't take long for some to be found.

Not paralyzed by fear, they serve others in stride
they're not hung up by ego or pride.

We can learn from them and the example they set they
keep doing for others without any regret.

So let's too work to be caring so that others may see
a supernatural hero reflected in you and in me.

Joseph M. Tabers © May 27, 2006

A FINAL CONSIDERATION...

G od puts it inside of each one of us to be heroic, that is, to be self-sacrificing for a higher good. And to be honest, you and I can even sense that we are at our best when we're serving others for the greater glory of God.

So, to help us serve others with good intent, consider making the following prayer, your prayer:

> *My God, I belong and always wish to belong to you, in suffering or in pain, in spiritual dryness or in joy, in illness or in health, in life or in death. I want only one thing: that your will be done in me and by me. More and more I seek, and desire to seek, only one end: to promote your greater glory through the accomplishment of your desires for me. Amen.*

Elisabeth Leseur (1866-1914)
French married lay woman
Her cause for canonization is underway

SUMMARIZING THE TAKEAWAYS

S o, in a nutshell: How do I Bloom Where I'm Planted?

REMEMBER:

✓ **God has given you a special grace** to use for the service of others.

✓ **We are at our best when serving others** for the greater glory of God.

✓ **The ideal job doesn't exist.** All work grows in value the more of your heart you put into it.

✓ **Sincerely serve someone,** and both you and they will feel better.

✓ **Make a positive difference!** Inconveniences or interruptions may be opportunities for you in disguise.

CHAPTER 6 ACTION TIPS:

◉ **Strive NOW** to do your present responsibilities to the best of your abilities.

◉ **Go the extra mile.** Get in the habit of going the extra mile, of doing more than you are paid for. You will enjoy yourself more and you may inspire others.

◉ **Become over-qualified** for your current role or tasks. When you grow in value, you add more value to whomever you serve.

PRACTICE PATIENCE AND PERSISTENCE; Eliminate Self-doubt

Patience and perseverance have a magical effect before which difficulties disappear and obstacles vanish.

> John Quincy Adams (1767–1848)
> Sixth President of the United States of America,
> from 1825 to 1929

The companion of patience is wisdom.

> Saint Augustine

Never think that God's delays are God's denials. Hold on; hold fast; hold out. Patience is genius.

> George Louis Leclerc de Buffon (1707–1788)
> Comte de Buffon, French naturalist,
> mathematician, cosmologist

Great works are performed, not by strength, but by perseverance.

> Dr. Samuel Johnson (1709–1784)
> English poet, critic, and essayist

HOW COMPELLED ARE YOU TO WORK TOWARD SOMETHING WORTHWHILE?

When I was in my late teens I dreamed of helping people using two of the ways that I personally had been influenced and helped the most; public speaking and writing.

When I asked myself "who influenced me the most?" the answer that most often came to mind was "good teachers, motivational speakers and generous book authors". It would be nearly five years later, at the age of 22, before I earned my first income (remember that $50 dollars I mentioned earlier?) from speaking to a student group about the power of purpose in life.

It would be another two years before I could earn enough to cut my full-time job in commercial building maintenance work down to part-time. And finally, by the age of 25 (it seemed to take forever at the time), I was able to earn enough from speaking to call it my full-time calling/career. By then I was truly learning the old adage that states: "Anything worth having, is worth working hard for."

Trust me, even though it sounds like no time at all when you read about it here in this book, everything seemed to take twice as long as I thought it should have taken at the time!

I would later discover that the same feeling, of having things take longer than I thought they should take, happens for almost everyone, regardless of their calling in life!

In the fast food, I-want-it-now, microwave-ready society in which we live, we risk getting conditioned to "having it our way"– what we want, when we want it, and how we want it - unless we're persistent in resisting the culture we live in.

But all we have to do is take a look around at what nature shows us to see that we don't control the universe. For example, it takes nine months of waiting before a baby is born (unless were talking about elephants which could take up to year of waiting before they give birth). The changing seasons transition over a period of several months every year. Farmers cannot skip steps from tilling the soil and planting the seeds, to watering, pest-control and eventually harvesting.

SO, WHY DO WE GET SO IMPATIENT, ESPECIALLY CONSIDERING THE WAY THINGS WORK IN NATURE?

We get impatient when we attempt to be in control of too many things instead of letting God be in control. This does not however mean giving up and passively sitting around waiting for God to "make it happen". The onset of hopelessness is caused by not sacrificing and not struggling toward a worthwhile goal that benefits others.

Never lose hope! Losing hope is never an option. We have to keep moving forward on worthwhile endeavors, especially when they're for the greater good of others or for the glory of God.

We have to be patient, yet persistent. Even if we fail or fall short, it is never too late to get up, get moving and begin again. God will supply the graces we need.

Even later, after we are feeling more confident in our calling, we can still experience those "don't bother" or "it's not worth it" feelings when we are working toward something worthwhile or on an important project.

For example, I have been a member of the National Speakers Association since 1983. In 1988 I set a goal to earn my Certified Speaking Professional designation (the CSP) in four years. I figured that by 1992 I would have met all the stringent requirements.

Well, lo and behold, 1992 came and went, and no CSP. The years 1993 and 1994 passed by in the same way. Finally, when I stopped fretting about making the certification happen and decided to just let it unfold in God's own time, I experienced a much greater sense of peace. When I finally did receive the CSP designation in 1998 I had really earned it in God's time, not mine.

In my travels and work with people in over 45 states and four countries, I have heard similar stories from dozens of other professionals. For example, people have talked to me about college degrees that have not taken the typical four years to earn, but may have taken six to 11 years or more to earn, because of different life events.

For others, it took five to more than 15 years before they found fulfilling work or a meaningful career, even though they thought it would have taken a much shorter time. In each person's life and in each instance, the important lesson remains true for all of us...**just because something takes longer to achieve does not mean we should just give up.**

Sometimes we just need to let go, do our part, and trust that God will work out the details...in His time frame not ours.

THE OPPOSITE OF PATIENCE AND PERSISTENCE

Not to be confused with a healthy sense of urgency, impatience can make us anxious and worried.

Pray, hope, and don't worry.
Worry adds nothing...

St. Padre Pio

I once heard that the devil's two main tools, which he loves to use, are:

DESPAIR (hopelessness, the "I can't do this, so why bother?" feeling)

PRIDE (defiant thinking such as, "I don't need God or any others.")

A Helpful Reminder for Increasing Patience, Persistence and Confidence:

Remember

that YOU ARE
a child of GOD.
It will give you a steady,
solid peace,
undisturbed
by the ups and downs
of daily life events.

IDENTIFY WHAT'S HOLDING YOU BACK

One of the best definitions of "luck" that I ever learned was when I was 18 years old. The definition read like this: **"Luck is nothing but preparation meeting opportunity."**

"Preparation meeting opportunity." In other words, if we are not prepared, we can't take advantage of opportunities that are all around us all the time.

I am convinced that one of worst things we can do is to allow negative self-talk (doubt) to dominate us. You know the kind of talk I mean: "I can't," "I'm too young," "I'm too old," "I'm too short," "I'm too tall," "I'm too this...I'm too that."

In the simple saying of a friend's father who grew up in a one-room house in the Alabama backwoods during the Depression, "Can't – never did do nuthin'!" True!

If you want to see a great example that will inspire you to never complain or make excuses again, go to YouTube or Google Videos and search for the "No Excuses" NIKE commercial. I believe this is one of the most inspiring short video commercials I have ever seen. I hope you agree!

If you have trouble finding the Nike "No Excuses" video, go to our website **www.GodHasGreatPlans.com** and we have a link for it there.

YOUR TURN /

A PROVEN APPROACH: DIVIDE AND CONQUER

Make a list, right now, of those things you fear or that are causing self-doubt. Then decide to DO something about them. Read a book on the topic. Take an online course or buy an audio CD. In other words, equip yourself to conquer the fear by learning more about it or improving your skills.

If we only did what's comfortable, we'd all stay in bed.

Mother Teresa of Calcutta understood this concept. People who visited her said that she had this poem on her wall:

DO IT ANYWAY

People are often unreasonable,
illogical, and self-centered;
forgive them anyway.

If you are kind,
people may accuse you of selfish,
ulterior motives;
be kind anyway.

If you are successful,
you will win some false friends
and some true enemies; succeed anyway.

If you are honest and frank,
people may cheat you;
be honest and frank anyway.

What you spend years building,
someone could destroy overnight;
build anyway.

If you find serenity and happiness,
there may be jealousy;
be happy anyway.

The good you do today,
people will often forget tomorrow;
do good anyway.

Give the world the best you have,
and it may never be enough;
give the world the best you've got anyway.

You see, in the final analysis,
it is between you and God;
it was never between you and them anyway.

Anonymous

NEVER, NEVER DESPAIR!

Be aware…the devil (who is very real, but ultimately not as powerful as God) uses excessive or misdirected pride to tempt us into paralysis or ineffective action (e.g., "I can do this myself…I don't need God").

When pride doesn't work, the devil tempts us to despair and hopelessness (e.g., *"I can't do anything…"* *"God and no one else cares, nothing matters."*)

Instead…

TAKE

COURAGE!

HAVE

FAITH!

Be at peace.

Know that God delights

in your ordinary, small works.

Listen carefully to the words of our Saviour:

> *I am the light of the world*
> *whoever follows me*
> *will have the light of life*
> *and will never walk in darkness.*
>
> Jesus Christ
> as recorded in John 8:12

And listen to what others say:

> *The most significant thing in our life right now is that Jesus is preparing us to enter into the presence of the Father! He is interceding for us in subduing everything that is in us that is opposed to the Father.*
>
> Peter Herbek, Renewal Ministries

Self-doubt paralyzes us.
But self-doubt is really fear.
Fear is useless...
WHAT IS NEEDED IS FAITH!

> *Pray, hope, and don't worry.*
> *Worry is useless.*
> *God is merciful and will hear your prayer.*
>
> Saint Padre Pio

WE WILL ALL HAVE DAYS OF SELF-DOUBT.
SELF-DOUBT IS A NORMAL PART OF ANY BIG PROJECT

One day I was contacted by an education director from a State Principals Association to speak at a regional conference for approximately 80 to 90 middle school principals. I had been heavily involved with customer service and customer service leadership training for several years at the time and they needed a speaker to address the principals on ways to inspire more "customer service thinking" in schools.

We talked for several minutes, they listened to the suggested approach I would take and we agreed on the date. I soon received a 50% deposit and a confirmation letter of agreement.

Then the fear set in. I found myself thinking "who am I to speak to these principals?" They all had at least a Masters Degree, many had earned a Ph.D., and I was a self-study guy who didn't even hold a college degree.

When I could sense the erroneous, crippling fear creeping in, I knew that I had to sit down and get hold of my thinking. So I did. I reminded myself that I was hired for what I knew and for the value I could bring to that audience, not for what I didn't know or didn't have.

Ultimately, I had to trust that God was putting me before this audience for a reason. Once I accepted this truth, then I prepared and looked forward to the event. The entire session went extremely well, with several principals saying it was one of the best sessions they had ever attended. I was greatful and humbled.

> At its **best**, self-doubt can make us **lean more**, and depend more, **upon God**.
>
> At its **worst**, self-doubt can immobilize us and **freeze** us from taking **action**.

Ford Motor Company Founder, Henry Ford once said:

Whether you think you can or think you can't, you're right.

Another one of my favorite poems follows. I remember when I first heard this poem I really, really liked it and it was easy for me to remember and share with others many times since.

HELP FOR STOPPING "IF ONLY I ..." THINKING

A t times, we can be our own worst critic and it can quickly lead to counter-productive thinking. When I came across this poem, I found it very helpful in stopping negative thinking. Maybe you will consider saving or sharing this poem with others as well.

THE VICTOR

If you think you are beaten, you are.
If you think you dare not, you don't.
If you like to win but think you can't,
It's almost a cinch you won't.

If you think you'll lose, you've lost.
For out in the world we find
Success begins with a fellow's will.
It's all in the state of mind.

If you think you're outclassed, you are.
You've got to think high to rise.
You've got to be sure of yourself before
You can ever win the prize.

Life's battles don't always go
To the stronger or faster man.
But sooner or later the man who wins,
Is the man who thinks he can.

C. W. Longenecker

SUMMARIZING THE TAKEAWAYS

S o, in a nutshell: how do I Eliminate Doubt and Practice Patience, and Persistence?

Remember:

✓ **Never lose hope.** Never give up.

✓ **Keep moving forward** on worthwhile endeavors, especially when they are for the greater good of others or for God.

✓ **When impatience rises, trust** that all good things happen in God's own time.

✓ **Look at nature** (and history) for reminders that all good things come to pass in time, not overnight.

✓ **Have faith! Be at peace.** You are a child of the Creator of the Universe!

Chapter 7 Action Tips:

○ **Practice hopefulness and trust**, not despair.

○ **Practice humility and gratitude**, not pride.

○ **Better equip yourself** for your current role or future tasks. Growing in value reduces fear and enables you to add more value to the lives of others.

WELCOME AND ENCOURAGE OTHERS
To Be at Their Best!

Everyone who has ever done a kind deed for us, or spoken a word of encouragement to us, has entered into the make-up of our character and our thoughts, as well as our success.

George Matthew Adams (1878-1962)

If something uncharitable is said in your presence, either speak in favor of the absent, or withdraw, or if possible, stop the conversation.

St John Vianney, Cure of Ars

Too often we underestimate the power of a touch, a smile, a kind word, a listening ear, an honest compliment, or the smallest act of caring, all of which have the potential to turn a life around.

Leo Buscaglia, writer

WELCOME AND ENCOURAGE OTHERS TO BE AT THEIR BEST!

A terrific priest in the Detroit area, Father John Ricardo, recently said: "One of the greatest crises of our time is a lack of love." Why do I bring this up in this chapter you might ask? Because one of the best definitions of love I've seen is "wanting the best for another person, another human being".

Love requires that we get outside of ourselves and do something for others, *without any want of return!*

To encourage someone is to want the best for that individual. It may include some of the following actions:

- Visiting them, especially the sick, elderly, lonely or abandoned

- Sharing your confidence in them

- Reminding them of their capabilities

- Reminding them of their past successes

- Reassuring them

- Helping them see the bigger picture

- Listening; being a sounding board for them

- Caring enough to confront them to do the right thing

- Talking them through irrational fears

- Praying for them or with them

- Lending a helping hand

When I was growing up. my mom and dad used to say: "If you put your mind to it, you can do anything!" Also, when I made mistakes or bad decisions, my dad was wise enough to say: "You know better than that!" "Come on...I didn't raise a dummy!" or "You're smarter than that...aren't you?"

Looking back on it, those words of confidence in me and encouragement meant an awful lot to me!

> *Kind words can be short and easy to speak,*
> *but their echoes are truly endless.*
>
> Mother Teresa

HOW TO BE AN ENCOURAGER...

Encouragement literally means to speak strength or courage into someone's life.

Most of us like being around people who share sincere, well-placed words of encouragement. Let people know when you believe in them or in their talents, skills, gifts or capabilities.

We can easily assume that others know their own strengths and miss seeing their weaknesses. We can even justify that when we point out another person's faults, we're just being helpful to them.

Well, "being helpful" might be our intent, but pointing out someone else's weaknesses usually isn't perceived as being very helpful. Instead of focusing on someone's weaknesses or need for improvement, work at sharing what you admire in their behavior or skills.

Find the good, and help it grow. Look for the spark or the glowing ember nestled among a person's ashes, and fan it into a beautiful, warmth-giving flame.

WHAT IF IT'S HARD TO SEE THE GOOD IN SOMEONE?

At the end of one of my workshops, a man named John came up to me and asked, "What if you've been severely hurt by someone close to you? How can you let go of the anger and resentment you still feel?" It was obvious that whatever had happened still affected this man greatly. He was tense and fighting bitterness. I listened to John talk for a long time and he said it helped just to talk about it.

We agreed that sometimes people close to you can hurt you so deeply that it is hard to let it go. We also agreed, if something that hurt you involved a crime, then it must be reported to the proper authorities so that such a person does not hurt others and, if possible, the criminal can pay restitution of some kind.

At the very least, reporting a criminal action might later prove to be the very catalyst the hurtful person needs to reform his (or her) life!

In John's case the hurt was caused by a deceased family member. To John's credit, he was wondering if forgiveness might help. And I agreed with him that I believe it would.

As human beings created in God's image, you and I have something of great value we can give. Forgiveness. Forgiveness, like encouragement, is a choice. It is your choice to do it, or not. It is your choice to forgive and move on, or to waste part of your life burning in resentment at someone or at circumstances that may not have been in your control in the first place. Forgiveness IS in your control. It is something that only you can choose to do.

Sometimes giving forgiveness takes awhile to process. It doesn't mean that you'd run out and do business with someone who already proved themselves untrustworthy. But it does mean that you let go of the resentment and anger you feel toward that person. You give that burden to God. Let the Creator of the universe, and of each one of us individually, make it right, in His own time. You and I have other things to do!

We don't give forgiveness because a hurtful person earned it. We can choose to give forgiveness because we choose to let the hurt go and move on.

To be an encourager, it helps if we tune in to others emotions.

THE GIFT OF ENCOURAGEMENT

In seventh grade I had an art teacher by the name of Mrs. Upton. That year I decided to make a huge cookie pot out of clay. It was so large you could stick a gallon jug of milk inside of it!

The problem was that as I was nearing completion and the clay still needed to be fired in the kiln, many of my snickering classmates began saying "That thing is so big, it will never survive the firing process! It will crack! It's too big!"

But my confidence remained unshaken.

You see, what my classmates did not realize is that in earlier classes that year, while I was building this monstrous cookie jar, Mrs. Upton encouraged me to make sure that all the air pockets were out of the clay as I built the jar. She convinced me that air pockets left in clay were the Number One reason why items cracked or exploded during the firing process. So I made double sure all air bubbles were out of that clay.

She was right! I listened. And my cookie pot survived the kiln, becoming a great Mother's Day gift that my mom treasured on her countertop for many years.

ARE YOU AN ENCOURAGER OR A DISCOURAGER?

Ask yourself:

- Do I help bring out the best in my friends and family members?

- Do I look for the good, the beauty, or the helpful intentions of other people? (even when I don't like some of their habits or imperfect behaviors)

I often tell my two growing sons:

> You are smarter than you know...
> and you are better than you think.
> **GOD** has big plans
> for **you!**

YOUR TURN /

GO ENCOURAGE SOMEONE NOW...AND TWO PEOPLE WILL FEEL BETTER BECAUSE OF IT.

> *Note how good you feel after you have encouraged someone else. No other argument is necessary to suggest that one should never miss the opportunity to give encouragement.*
>
> George Matthew Adams (1878-1962)

On what might **you encourage others?**

- Virtues

- Virtuous living

- Doing the right thing

- Taking the high road

- Helping others

- Sticking with something worth while

- Not giving up

How can I **encourage** another person?

- Always be ready to assist

- Pray first

- Smile

- Take notice of others/ be attentive

- Compliment others' work or efforts

- Ask others how they are doing or how you can help

- Send a thank you or thinking of you card

- Make a phone call to say hello or to catch up

- E-mail a family photograph or article to someone

- Stop by a neighbors house

- Bring someone a little unexpected snack or treat

- Volunteer your time or skills to worthy cause

Stay open to opportunities to be encouraging and helpful to those around you. Even when you're in a department store or business, if someone should ask you, "Do you work here?" You might try answering "No, I don't. But maybe I can help you."

  – Never miss an opportunity to let someone know
    verbally that they are good at what they do.

  – Share that you noticed and appreciated their
    extra efforts.

On the next page is another one of my favorite poems. As you may have noticed, I like to write poetry. Some of the poems I use in my public speaking are included in this book.

Also, part of my passion is collecting researched data about happiness, in order to help people who don't have faith to draw closer to faith. One of the themes of my professional workshops is "selflessness". I wanted a poem on this topic that would be appropriate for my professional audiences. And after several versions, the following poem emerged and has been very well received with a variety of audiences. I hope you will enjoy it too!

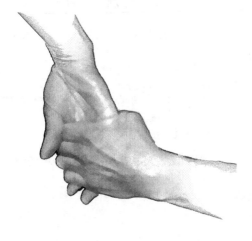

REAL JOY

In the giving of ourselves
that's where we find real joy.
It doesn't come from wealth or fame
or from buying another "toy".

It doesn't come from selfish acts
nor from owning the latest fashion,
but from sharing with others who need our time
and showing them some compassion.

We can work real hard to "make a mark"
but that's no guarantee...
of peace and joy within our heart
that shines for all to see.

Oh sure there are some selfish things
that can fool us into thinking
that joy is self-made like a high
some get from drugs or drinking.

And yes it's tempting to give in
to want to "get" and not to give,
but a look around at other's needs
will tell us, that's not how to live.

So if we truly want to make
a difference and a living,
we'll find the greatest joys in life
always come with selfless giving.

Joseph M. Tabers ©1992

WE NEED EACH OTHER!

We are all on a journey and heaven is our desired destination. As St. Augustine once wrote: "Our hearts are restless, O Lord, until they rest in thee."

God gave us each other so we can help each other along the way.

Here are some simple ways we can begin to help others:

- Live in our own lives the virtues and habits that inspire others.

- Encourage others to use and share their gifts.

- Pray for the gift of faith for others you know and love.

- Discourage selfishness.

- Encourage generosity.

ENCOURAGING OTHERS IS PART OF GOD'S PLAN

We all get tired. We all get frustrated at times. We all have days when things aren't going the way we planned. Well the same is true for every other person in the world too! Truly, we never know when another person may need some encouragement or a little bit of help to carry on.

For example, I volunteer as a facilitator of a large marriage preparation program five to six times per year for couples engaged to be married. At these weekends we have volunteer guest speakers who address helpful marriage preparation topics. Well, one particular Saturday morning after an unusually long and busy week for me, I was feeling extremely tired. I explained this to Gordon, a guest speaker who was a newer volunteer at the time.

Immediately he took the initiative and said "No problem Joe... What can I do to help?" Within minutes I felt overwhelmingly grateful for his timely offer of help, assistance and energy! Gordon's simple offer of help had really lifted my spirits that day!

Gordon's generous spirit, and his spontaneous offer to help, made God's grace and mercy very visible to me that morning. The weekend was a great success and I was extremely relieved and thankful that I didn't have to do it all myself!

We all need encouragement. We all need the help or assistance of others. When you feel you can't go on, ask God and the people He places around you for some help. More often than not, family, friends and even strangers will gladly lend a hand. I have witnessed it many times.

Humility is not only in asking for help, but it is also in gracefully accepting and receiving help from others. That means, getting our pride out of the way to ask for, and accept, help!

ENCOURAGEMENT

You are better than
- and more capable than -
you think you are!

You are a Son or Daughter of God!

Right now, you can
do something that
helps other people.

Ask, who can use my help
or assistance right now?

Then...Go do it!

YOUR TURN /

To keep yourself inspired, start today to collect and more importantly, to display words of encouragement for yourself, your family, your friends and acquaintances.

These following two pages can help you get started.

NEVER UNDERESTIMATE THE POWER OF ENCOURAGEMENT

> One of the highest of human duties is the duty of encouragement...It is easy to laugh at men's ideals; it is easy to pour cold water on their enthusiasm; it is easy to discourage others. The world is full of discouragers. We have a Christian duty to encourage one another. Many a time a word of praise or thanks or appreciation or cheer has kept a man on his feet. Blessed is the one who speaks such a word.

> William Barclay
> Scottish scholar

People can reduce their negative self-talk or self-criticism through encouragement. **People can be healed by encouragement**; they can grow to like themselves and to act in healthier ways if they're encouraged.

> If one part of Christ's body is praised, all the other parts share its happiness.
>
> 1 Corinthians 12:26

> He who refreshes others will himself be refreshed.
>
> Proverbs 11:25

> Therefore encourage one another and build up one another...
>
> 1 Thessalonians 5:11

Yes, It is within our power to build each other up with words of encouragement.

The Scripture verse of Proverbs 3:27 talks about looking for opportunities to help and bless, because it's in our power to do so:

> *Do not withhold good from those to whom it is due,*
> *when it is in your power to do it.*
>
> Proverbs 3:27

And, Proverbs 16:24 tells us that pleasant words are sweet to the soul and health to the bones:

> *Pleasant words are a honeycomb,*
> *sweet to the soul and healing to the bones.*
>
> Proverbs 16:24

Proverbs 25:11 reminds us that a word aptly spoken is as precious as silver and gold! Wow!

> *Like apples of gold in settings of silver*
> *is a word spoken in right circumstances.*
>
> Proverbs 25:11

Encouragement is a basic human need. Each one of us likes to feel important and to have our work or efforts recognized and appreciated.

Encourage the people around you today, for you never know what they're going through or how much they may need that simple gift of your encouragement!

Some encouraging reminders:

> *Since we have gifts that differ according to the grace given to us, each of us is to exercise them accordingly: if prophecy, according to the proportion of his faith; if service, in his serving; or he who teaches, in his teaching; or he who exhorts, in his exhortation; he who gives, with liberality; he who leads, with diligence; he who shows mercy, with cheerfulness. Let love be without hypocrisy. Abhor what is evil; cling to what is good.*
>
> Romans 12: 6-9

But encourage one another day after day, as long as it is still called "Today," so that none of you will be hardened by the deceitfulness of sin...

Hebrews 3:13

Therefore if there is any encouragement in Christ,
if there is any consolation of love,
if there is any fellowship of the Spirit,
if any affection and compassion,
make my joy complete by being of the same mind,
maintaining the same love,
united in spirit, intent on one purpose.

Do nothing from selfishness or empty conceit,
but with humility of mind regard one another
as more important than yourselves;
do not merely look out for your own personal interests,
but also for the interests of others.

Have this attitude in yourselves which was also in Christ Jesus,

Philippians 2:1-5

And let us consider how we may spur one another on toward love and good deeds.

Hebrews 10:24

Two Helpful Formats for Practicing Encouragement
Simple as 1 – 2 – 3

FORMAT # 1:

NAME OF PERSON: _____

1. STATE POSITIVE BEHAVIOR...   1. _____
   Be specific and detailed.
   " I really appreciate your..."   _____

2. EXPLAIN HOW POSITIVE   2. _____
   BEHAVIOR IMPACTS...
   Explain how it impacts you,   _____
   another person, or a whole group

3. THANK THEM AGAIN (BY NAME)   3. _____
   Thank them for taking time
   and making the effort   _____

EXAMPLE:

Peter, your thoughtfulness in helping us clean up after the party was really appreciated! It would have taken much longer without all of your generous help, plus you inspired others to assist. Thanks again Peter for sharing your time to help out.

Recognition, appreciation, and encouragement can really help others to get and stay motivated.

FORMAT #2:

NAME OF PERSON: _____

ONE (OR TWO) OF THE THINGS I REALLY...
   (select one of the following:)
                              . ADMIRE
                              . RESPECT
                              . APPRECIATE
                              . NOTICE/SENSE
                              . LOVE

...ABOUT YOU IS/ARE... _____

EXAMPLE:

Eva, two of the things I admire about you, are your patience and your desire to do quality work.

The <u>best time</u> to show your appreciation to someone...is NOW.

SUMMARIZING THE TAKEAWAYS

S o, in a nutshell: How do I welcome and encourage others to be at their best?

Remember:

✓ **Every one of us has been helped** or shaped by another person's encouragement for us.

✓ **Encouragement helps** to bring out, or reinforce the best in ourselves and in others.

✓ **Look for the good in others.** Choose to focus on the strengths, talents, skills and abilities of others.

Chapter 8 Action Tips:

⊙ **Choose one.** Review the second page of this chapter and select one encouragement action that you can commit to doing within 24 hours.

⊙ **Begin to collect, display and read** words of encouragement in your home, work or study area.

⊙ **Encourage someone today.** Speak strength, courage or reinforcement into someone's life. Practice using one of the helpful formats on page 133 to collect your thoughts.

⊙ **Do it!** Don't wait! Get up and go, or pick up the phone! Actions speak louder than words.

Conclusion

GO FORTH!

As stated at the beginning, this book was created to help you get a jump-start in discovering the type of vocation and work God may be drawing you toward. The second goal of the book was to assist you, a friend or family member, in learning more about your unique strengths, dreams and capabilities so that you may grow into the best person God wants you to be!

My sincere prayer is that some of the contents of this book will have helped in that regard. Never doubt this fact; you make, and you are meant to make, a difference in this world. Know that God loves you, trust in Him and do your best with whatever work or responsibility is in front of you right now.

A QUICK RETURN ON YOUR READING INVESTMENT...

If you do nothing else, and yet you want to make a quick difference this very day, consider doing one or more of the following:

- Tear out or copy the summarizing page of each of the eight chapters (the one with Reminders and Action tips) then review them at least once more. Recall and repetition leads to application.

- Get yourself inspired and stay inspired by committing to a lifetime of service that benefits other people with the skills and gifts you've been given.
- Provide encouragement, inspiration and answers to help someone else by giving them a copy of this book.

Remember, GREAT plans usually require sacrifice – giving of ourselves beyond our "comfort zones". But please don't be quick to dismiss sacrifice as a bad thing!

Sacrifice is one of the noblest, most magnanimous things we can do when it is directed toward a greater good. For example, consider a firefighter, risking his or her life for the good of another, or a mother who might endure months of discomfort before child birth. Sacrifice for the sake of achieving a higher and noble good, is always a good and healthy thing.

Even great athletes sacrifice long training hours, day after day, month after month, sometimes for years, often doing what might seem like boring and grueling exercises, until eventually the skill and ability they seek becomes second nature. They become a valuable player on a sports team, or in an individual sport like tennis or running. To an unknowing spectator, a great athlete just seems to walk onto the field and do amazing things. But to a wise spectator, these athletic feats are remarkable for the amount of  self-discipline and determination that went on "behind the scenes" leading up to the big game or athletic event. Most of us don't see the days, months and sometimes years of sacrifice it took for the athlete to be able to do amazing things in his or her sport! Yet, we all like seeing top performers in action.

Anything worthwhile requires some sacrifice to achieve it. And the sacrifice is always worth it when it's for love of God or neighbor.

In truth, we can only follow Christ through a life of sacrifice – a sacrifice of our will, passions and desires. "Take up your cross and follow me," our loving Savior invites us. We can't do this without embracing sacrifice. Sacrifice makes sense, and can even be exciting when we know it's for the joy of living life forever with Our Lord and the saints in Heaven.

To put it simply...

Like many good things in life:
No pain, No gain.

It is in sufferings that our soul finds its full identification with Christ.

It is not possible to follow our Lord without the cross.

Sacrifice and pain bring us closer to CHRIST our REDEEMER.

If we really want to bear fruit, love God, and help others in a great way...Sacrifice will be a necessary but doable part of the package.

Mortification frees us from things that tie us down, and gives us a greater capacity to love. Mortification means to purposefully deny ourselves some little comfort for something greater.

For example, offering up our sacrifice for the Souls in Purgatory, for a loved one who is struggling, or for whoever (in our circle of relationships) needs our prayers the most.

Yes, we can do a lot of good in the world today by just "offering it up" like this. Even something as simple a sacrifice of choosing to do our homework early, instead of at the last minute, is something that we can "offer up" for a higher good. That's pretty powerful, isn't it?!

Never doubt the value of prayers and sacrifice before making important decisions or taking action. In John 15:16, Jesus tells us:

> *You have not chosen me; I have chosen you.*
> *Go and bear fruit that will last.*

BE A LIGHT FOR OTHERS!

Everyone of us was born for a reason. After reading and doing the exercises in this little book, challenge yourself to be the best person God wants you to be! Each of us has a purpose and mission to accomplish during our life time. If you have read this far and have implemented some of the suggested action tips; you are already well on your way to living and continuously discovering God's will for you.

By living this way, and by keeping our eyes and ears on Jesus, we automatically become shining lights for others that are much needed in our world today.

> *The Lord is always calling us to come out of ourselves and to share with others the goods we possess, starting with the most precious gift of all – our faith.*
>
> Pope John Paul II, Mission of the Redeemer, 49

GO FORTH!

Now the next steps are up to you on your exciting journey! Simply striving to know and to do God's will, does bear fruit. Yes, God indeed has great plans *for* YOU! Enjoy the journey!

We will be adding additional resources to assist you on the website at **www.GodHasGreatPlans.com**

ONE MORE THING...

If you can carve out a quick moment, drop me a line or email. Let me know if this little book has helped you in any way. Also if you have suggestions on ways we can help more people with this book or with future products, please let us know.

The fine people who helped put this book together pray every day for each person who reads it. That means you! Please pray for us too.

I'd love to hear from you!

Joe Tabers

joe@GodHasGreatPlans.com

P.O. Box 130857
Ann Arbor, MI 48113

About the author...

Joseph Michael Tabers was born in Detroit, Michigan, March of 1959. He is a son of two terrific parents, a brother of five wonderful siblings, a husband of a fantastic wife, a dad to two great boys, an uncle, neighbor, friend, a Catholic Christian and so much more.

From his parent's example, Joe learned the importance of faith in God and relationship with God. In his own words, he says, "It was through my parents that I first learned that God is real – a real, living person – and that Jesus Christ IS God. I discovered that in knowing Jesus, I can actually know God as truly as I know any of my family or friends. Later on, as an adult, I did my own exhaustive comparative religion studies only to arrive at the same amazing conclusion!"

Joe adds: "When we're growing up and maturing as young adults, it can take some time to fully understand the gifts we've been given (for example, the gift of faith). I know it took me awhile to fully understand the Scripture verse *'Seek first the kingdom of God and all else will be given in addition'*. Today I am a grateful, faith-filled Catholic man who loves and appreciates my faith and the relationship I have with our Lord Jesus Christ."

It is through this Catholic Christian lens, as well as through the lens of 50 years of life experience, miles of travels, and working with people in all walks of life, that Joe wrote this book.

Having earned distinction as a Certified Speaking Professional (CSP) by the National Speakers Association in 1998, Joe continues to write and lecture on workplace leadership, trust and teamwork. He passionately works with up to 100 audiences per year.

For information regarding Joe's availability as a speaker for your group or organization, contact his office at:

Productive Training Services,
Inc.P.O. Box 130857
Ann Arbor, MI 48113
Phone: 1- 800-805-8780
Or visit them on the web at www.ProductiveTraining.com